DISCOVER

music of the
Baroque Era

by

Clive Unger-Hamilton

D1498652

Published by Naxos Books, an imprint of Naxos Rights International Ltd
© Naxos Books 2007
www.naxosbooks.com

Printed and bound in China by Leo Paper Group
Design and layout: Hannah Davies, Fruition – Creative Concepts
Music compiled by Clive Unger-Hamilton
Editors: Harriet Smith, Ingalo Thomson
Map illustrator: Arthur Ka Wai Jenkins
Timeline: Hugh Griffith
All photographs © AKG Images unless otherwise credited

Front cover score extract: The beginning of J.S. Bach's Violin Sonata No. 1
in G minor, BWV 1001 in the composer's own hand

A CIP Record for this book is available from the British Library.

All rights reserved. No part of this publication may be reproduced, stored in
a retrieval system, or transmitted in any form or by any means, electronic,
mechanical, photocopying, recording or otherwise, without the prior written
permission of Naxos Rights International Ltd.

ISBN: 978-1-84379-234-5

Contents

Website

Log onto **www.naxos.com/naxosbooks/discoverbaroque**
and hear over two hours of music, all referred to in the text.

To access the website you will need:

ISBN: 9781843792345
Password: Telemann

website Streamed at 64Kbps to provide good-quality sound.

website Easy links to view and purchase any of the original
CDs from which the extracts are taken.

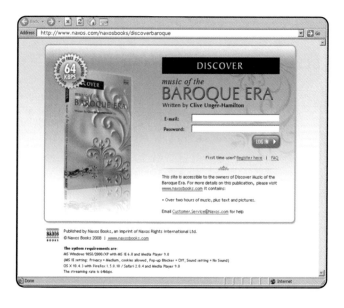

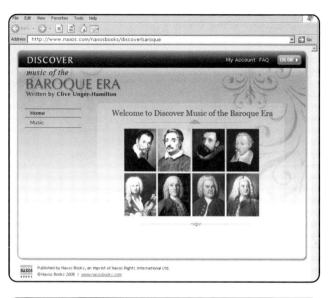

music of the
Baroque Era

by

Clive Unger-Hamilton

*Allegory of the friendship between Buxtehude (with the sheet of
music) and Hamburg colleagues from St Katharinen,
Johann Adam Reincken (at the harpsichord) and Johann Theile.
Painting, 1674, by Johannes Voorhout (1647–1723)*

I. Introduction: Enter the Players

What is Baroque music? Historically it is fairly easy to define, flourishing between about 1600 and 1750. Its opening date coincides almost exactly with the 'invention' of opera, while its closing date is that of the death of the era's musical superhero, Johann Sebastian Bach. But unlike other artistic periods, stylistically the Baroque is almost impossible to define, since its chief characteristic was an astonishing variety of ideas coupled with a compelling urge to communicate them. The word 'baroque' means oddly or eccentrically shaped, which might seem difficult to apply to music; but if you can bend those adjectives to give them a sense that includes words like 'brilliant' and 'extravagant', then the definition becomes more meaningful. It was certainly an age of virtuosity and ostentatiousness: look at the way people decorated their churches, their carriages, their houses – and also themselves.

Then, as now, there was an extraordinary amount of music around – the difference being that in those days it was all live. Already, for some hundreds of years, educated people had been expected to be able to sing music reasonably well at sight and to play at least one instrument competently. Not being able to do either of these things constituted a serious social gaffe, as the English composer Thomas Morley noted in his *A Plaine and Easie Introduction to Practicall Musicke* of 1597:

> Supper being ended, the musicke bookes (according to the custome) being brought to the table, the mistress of the house presented mee with a part, earnestly requesting me to sing, but when, after many excuses, I protested unfeignedly that I could not, everie one began to wonder, yea, some whispered to others, demaunding how I was brought up.

Individuality

One trend above all marked a break from the old style of music: the emergence of the soloist, and with it a corresponding culture of virtuosity. The fifteenth century, and the first half of the sixteenth, had been filled largely with musicians who sang or played together on equal terms – as part of a balanced polyphony. The great masses of such masters as William Byrd, Palestrina and others, woven into complicated webs of sound and gravely beautiful in effect, were essentially a united chorus of praise to Heaven; each voice was no less and no more important than all the others. Superficially, the devotional choral music of Byrd and Palestrina, for example, sounds quite similar, even though one composer was in England and the other in Italy.

The transformation of the composer's role from that of a jobbing worker into a recognisable creative voice took place around the close of a century that had seen the greatest changes in Europe since it emerged from the Dark Ages. Thanks to the invention of printing, music ceased to be the exclusive preserve of scholarly monks and became much more widely available.

Italy: the Cradle of the Baroque

Much of the new music was first found in Italy, not yet a unified country at the opening of the seventeenth century but a collection of independent states ruled by great and ancient families who spent their time in perpetual rivalry. However, so strong was Italy's cultural influence that its language has remained the *lingua franca* of music ever since. Four words – sonata, cantata, opera and concerto – are particularly significant in this context since they indicate the direction that music was to take for at least the next 300 years. 'Sonata', meaning 'sounded' (i.e. played), was at first simply an instruction or definition to distinguish instrumental music from that which was 'cantata' or 'sung'. 'Opera' was at first purely a collection of linked pieces, some sung and some played, assembled to form a musical drama; while the original concept of 'concerto' was of one soloist or group of instruments pitted against another, larger musical force. In the hands of great masters, such definitions became greatly modified and expanded. The simple forms of concerted music written around 1600, for example, had by the end of the era developed into such undisputed masterpieces as Bach's Brandenburg Concertos, Vivaldi's *Four Seasons*, or the Twelve Grand Concertos, Op. 6 (website 1) that Handel wrote in London in the autumn of 1739.

Instrumental Development and Choral Virtuosity

It was not only musical style that was developing rapidly: technology grew apace throughout the period as well. Instruments became more powerful, more responsive, and keyboard instruments gradually increased in range. Short dances for lute, keyboard, wind or strings written at the start of the Baroque would, by the end of the period, have evolved into complex, lengthy and virtuoso suites for solo or accompanied instruments (website 2).

This change is especially dramatic in keyboard music: little country dances and song arrangements developed into larger-scale works such as the preludes and fugues, partitas and suites of J.S. Bach and the extraordinary, witty and glittering sonatas of Domenico Scarlatti (website 3).

Many regard the choral music of J.S. Bach – his Passions and cantatas – as the pinnacle of music; confronted with such masterpieces as his Mass in B minor and *St Matthew Passion* it is an argument impossible to refute. With over 150 years of different styles and developments to draw upon, Bach assembled Italian, German, French and other influences into a style he made completely his own (website 4).

This evolutionary process makes for a fascinating story, involving some of the greatest composers who ever lived. Above all, it is a history of people. It is time to go back to the early seventeenth century, the beginning of the Baroque era, when an Italian priest and composer named Gregorio Allegri was in Rome working for Pope Urban VIII. A setting of the *Miserere* website 5 he wrote for performance in the Sistine Chapel of the Vatican illustrates perfectly how the virtuoso soloist was beginning to intrude on the traditional balance of equal voices raised in praise together.

*The beginning of J.S. Bach's Violin Sonata No. 1 in G minor,
BWV 1001 in the composer's own hand*

II. The Beginnings

Gregorio Allegri (1582–1652)

Italy

Gregorio Allegri (1582–1652)
Giovanni Gabrieli (1554/7–1612)

Allegri was born in Rome where he worked for much of
his life, and he stands at the gateway to the age of the
Baroque. His famous *Miserere*, with its shatteringly high
treble part (these days a much sought-after solo for any
boy chorister), is written for two choirs which act like
opposing sections of an orchestra. It is a technique that
Allegri may have picked up from the illustrious musical
Gabrieli family, who worked predominantly at St Mark's
Cathedral in Venice. Giovanni Gabrieli, the most
illustrious member of the dynasty, was the nephew of
Andrea Gabrieli, organist at St Mark's. When Giovanni
was appointed to the post on his uncle's death in 1586,
so prestigious was the job that he immediately became
one of the most important musicians in the world.

Gabrieli wrote for instruments as if they were voices,
using the two-choir effect popularised in Venice by the
Flemish Adrian Willaert. He gave composers two things:
firstly a dramatic new vocabulary to use in creating a wider
range of sound; secondly the words 'sonata' and 'concerto'.
St Mark's resounded with the amazing new timbres of
double brass choirs (two separate groups of instruments in
different parts of the building), creating a thrilling
stereophonic effect that was enriched by Gabrieli's
innovation of putting directions in the score as to where
and when the music should be played loud (*forte*) or soft
(*piano*). It is something we take for granted these days but at

A visiting Englishman reports on a Vespers service at St Mark's, Venice:

'Upon St Roche's Day, I heard the best music that ever I did in all my life both in the morning and the afternoon, so good that I would willingly go 100 miles on foot at any time to hear the like. This feast consisted principally of music which was both vocal and instrumental, so good, so delectable, so rare, so admirable, so super excellent, that it did even ravish and stupefy all those strangers that never heard the like. But how others were affected with it I know not; for mine own part I can say this, that I was for the time even rapt up with Saint Paul into the third heaven.'

the time it was a huge step forward. Composers from all over Europe flocked to hear the new sounds and to learn from them, two of the most important being Claudio Monteverdi and the German Heinrich Schütz: 'Ye Gods, what a man was this!' said the latter of the great Venetian. One of Gabrieli's most famous works, the *Sonata pian' e forte* website 6 of 1597, clearly shows the revolutionary effects he introduced, and just as clearly demonstrates why Schütz so revered the genius who was his teacher.

Claudio Monteverdi (1567–1643)

The contribution to music of the next great Italian composer, Claudio Monteverdi, with his mastery of many genres and his almost single-handed invention of opera, places him in the very highest rank of musicians, alongside Bach and Mozart. Born in Cremona, the son of a barber-surgeon, he was taught music privately, learning several instruments including the organ. His promise showed early, and his first pieces were published when he was only fifteen – a collection of unaccompanied motets for three voices.

Monteverdi's career took a leap forward when in 1590 his talent was spotted at the princely court of Vincenzo Gonzaga, Duke of Mantua in Milan. Gonzaga employed him as singer and viol player; and, as one of the key musicians in the court, Monteverdi accompanied Gonzaga on a military campaign against the Turks in Hungary, and later on a diplomatic mission to the Low Countries. In 1599 Monteverdi married Claudia, a court singer from Mantua,

Claudio Monteverdi (1567–1643)

**"Claudio Monteverdi, in moving the affections...
becomes the most pleasant tyrant of human minds."**

Aquilino Coppini, in 1608,
quoted in Stravinsky's *Themes and Conclusions* (1972)

and was soon widely appreciated as a composer thanks to the publication of several books of highly original madrigals.

The year 1607 was highly significant, not just for Monteverdi but for musical history, as it marked the staging of Monteverdi's first opera, *Orfeo*, in Mantua. It was not in fact the world's earliest opera: the Italians Jacopo Peri and Giulio Caccini had pipped him to the post. But these lightweight pieces are not in the same league, and only survive in music history books because of their proximity to the pastoral *Orfeo*. Monteverdi was the first to create a real three-dimensional dramatic relationship between words and music, choosing the popular legend of Orpheus and Eurydice as his subject. His duties as court musician in Mantua included writing music for the church, and *Vespers of the Blessed Virgin* (website 7), his 1610 setting of the Vespers, is perhaps his best-known composition today. Its opening chorus with instruments ('God, make speed to help me. Lord, make haste to help me. Glory be to the Father' etc.) creates a magnificent uplifting sound, and shows how much from Gabrieli's ground-breaking techniques Monteverdi had absorbed.

When Monteverdi's patron died in 1612 the composer was lucky enough to land the job of *maestro di cappella* at St Mark's, Venice, in succession to Gabrieli. Here he spent the last thirty years of his life and wrote at least a dozen more operas. One of them, *L'incoronazione di Poppea* (1642), has survived in its complete form (unlike most of his others) and now enjoys a firm foothold in the repertoire.

On his death in 1643 Monteverdi was buried in the Venetian church of the Fratri, leaving a legacy that had

The newness of Monteverdi's musical style did not meet with universal approval. One of his most public detractors was a contemporary theorist called Giovanni Maria Artusi who, in 1600, wrote a book entitled *The Imperfection of Modern Music*. Though Monteverdi was not mentioned by name, his works come in for vicious attack, with quotations from several of his madrigals. When the composer published his next collection of madrigals, his preface most eloquently hit back:

'Do not wonder that I am allowing these madrigals to be printed without first replying to the attacks which Artusi has made against certain short passages in them. Since being in the service of His Serene Highness of Mantua I have not the time which would be required to do so; I have nevertheless written a reply to make known that I do not compose haphazardly, and as soon as it is rewritten it will be published bearing the title Second Practice or On the Perfection of Modern Music, which will perhaps surprise those who do not believe that there is any other way of composition save that taught by Zarlino; but let them be assured that, with regard to consonances and dissonances, there is yet another consideration different from those usually held, which defends the modern method of composition while giving satisfaction to the reason and the senses, and this I have wished to say, so that this expression 'second practice' may not be used by anyone else and the ingenious may reflect upon other secondary matters concerning music, and believe that the modern composer builds upon the foundations of truth.'

changed music for ever. Not only had he established opera as a dramatic form but his imaginative and innovative approach to instrumental music was hugely influential, including the introduction of new orchestral effects such as *pizzicato* and *tremolo* strings.

One area that Monteverdi left virtually untouched was the keyboard, whether organ or harpsichord. Idiomatic keyboard styles such as the Italian or the French were still in their infancy, at least in southern Europe. The first great Italian master of the medium, and an important influence on generations of later keyboard composers extending right down to J.S. Bach and beyond, was Girolamo Frescobaldi.

Girolamo Frescobaldi (1583–1643)

Born in Ferrara, at that time an important musical centre, Frescobaldi studied in his native city and became organist in one of its local churches when he was just fourteen. In 1607 he was appointed organist at the lovely church of Santa Maria de Trastevere in Rome, and also made a protracted trip to Brussels and probably Antwerp too, where his first book of madrigals was published in 1608. Returning to Rome, he was soon appointed to the prestigious position of organist at St Peter's, where he was to remain for the rest of his life (apart from a five-year spell working for the great Medici family in Florence).

Though his music can today seem rather antiquated and inflexible on first hearing, its rhythmic invention, lively melodic sense and use of jarring dissonance were to prove epoch-making in the early seventeenth century; and, thanks

Girolamo Frescobaldi (1583–1643)

to his publications as well as reports of his legendary playing, he was famous throughout Europe. Among his numerous collections of keyboard pieces, a set of ricercare published in Rome is especially attractive, having an intimacy, warmth and wit that is sometimes in short supply in music of this period.

Music in Colder Climates

Leaving Frescobaldi in Rome, it is time to make a journey north across Europe to Belgium and Holland – or the Low Countries, as they were then known. This small corner of the continent had long enjoyed a high musical reputation, partly thanks to a well-established school of organ and harpsichord builders. Its most important craftsman, Hans Ruckers of Antwerp (c. 1555–1598), made instruments of unsurpassed sonority, beauty and precision, and he was known as the Stradivari of the keyboard. Some of his instruments have survived and are still in use today.

Over in England, there had been a flourishing tradition of keyboard playing from as far back as the reign of King Henry VIII. Mary, Queen of Scots and her cousin Elizabeth were both accomplished players. The music of William Byrd, Orlando Gibbons and others was widely renowned, and the finest composer–performer of them all, John Bull, took refuge in the Low Countries early in the seventeenth century following some offence committed in England (probably adultery). In 1617 he became organist at Antwerp Cathedral, where he befriended a fascinating figure in early Baroque keyboard circles: Sweelinck.

Jan Pieterszoon Sweelinck (1562–1621)

Jan Pieterszoon Sweelinck (1562–1621)

For all Sweelinck's importance in the musical history books, his life was outwardly pretty humdrum. Born in Amsterdam, he spent all his fifty-nine years there, making only occasional trips to visit friends and colleagues in nearby cities. But this parochial existence did not prevent him from becoming famed throughout Europe as a composer and a performer. While still in his teens he became organist at the famous 'Old Church' in Amsterdam, a post previously held by his father. There he remained for the rest of his life, writing prodigious quantities of *chansons*, sacred songs and psalm settings.

But it was his keyboard works that brought him international fame, especially his sets of variations, which are still delighting players and audiences over 400 years later. One of them, a set of six Variations on *Mein junges Leben hat ein End* ('My Young Life Has an End' website 8), a popular German song of the time, is especially beguiling, with its opening scale figure popping up at the beginning of each variation like a visit from an old friend.

As well as being an outstanding composer and performer, Sweelinck was also renowned as an exceptional teacher. The published compositions one of the greatest of his pupils, Samuel Scheidt, were to have an important influence on the young J.S. Bach.

Samuel Scheidt (1587–1654)

Scheidt was born and died at Halle in Saxony (also the birthplace of Handel, in 1685), where his father was a beer and wine steward. When he was a youth he went to Amsterdam for lessons from Sweelinck, and on his return in 1609 Scheidt started work first as organist and later as director of music to the Margrave of Brandenburg. But these were troubled times, and when in 1625 his employer left for Denmark to fight for the Protestant cause Scheidt was stuck in his job without pay, undergoing much hardship and supporting himself as best he could by teaching. He is remembered today for the imaginative way in which he exploited the musical possibilities of Lutheran chorales, by extending, decorating and varying them, an idea that was to fascinate Bach.

Michael Praetorius (c. 1571–1621)

It comes as something of a relief to discover that music of an altogether lighter hue was also being written in Germany at this time! Michael Praetorius (his actual surname was Schultheiss which means 'magistrate', and as a young man he simply Latinised the word to Praetorius) was the son of a pastor in Thuringia. He studied philosophy and theology at Frankfurt University before entering the service of the powerful Duke of Brunswick as organist at his family seat in Wolfenbüttel. This was to remain the composer's base for the rest of his life, although during a spell in Dresden he did get to know the great choral composer Heinrich Schütz.

In the year 1610 a French musician by the name of Caroubel turned up in Wolfenbüttel on a visit from the court of the French king Henri IV at the Louvre. From him, the rather isolated Praetorius learned many of the songs and dances then in vogue among the Parisian smart set, which he transcribed and adapted. His collection of more than 300 pieces entitled *Terpsichore* contains Praetorius's own music as well as works by composers he had discovered through Caroubel. One of the French musicians whose work is featured here was a Parisian from earlier days, Pierre Certon (d. 1537). He worked as a lay clerk (adult chorister) at Notre Dame but had got into hot water with the authorities in 1529, being caught playing ball outside the cathedral when he should have been inside singing Mass. One of his songs, *La, la, la, je ne l'ose dire* ('Goodness Gracious, I Dare Not Tell You' website 9), complete with an instrumental variation, is as catchy now as it must have been then.

Heinrich Schütz (1585–1672)

The gloriously named Heinrich Sagittarius Schütz must rank as the greatest composer of Lutheran liturgical music before J.S. Bach, and indeed he wrote little else. His importance derives partly from the fusion of his native, rather academic, German style with Italian methods that he learned abroad, but also from an acute sensitivity to the words he was setting: his extensive choral works the *Christmas Story* and the *Seven Last Words on the Cross* glow with the fervour of a profound religious zeal.

Schütz was the son of a well-to-do innkeeper in Saxony. His family were opposed to a career in music, but as a youth he had shown such promise at studies in Hesse-Kassel that the ruler of the state, Landgrave Moritz, brought him to his court in Kassel and later paid for him to go to Venice for

Heinrich Schütz (1585–1672)

**"The most spiritual musician
the world has ever seen."**

Alfred Einstein, *Heinrich Schütz* (1928)

further study with the musical hero of the day, Giovanni
Gabrieli. Schütz was to spend almost four years in the Italian
city, returning to Germany only on his teacher's death in 1612.

The following year he took up the post of assistant organist
offered by his patron and was perfectly content – but it was
not to last. The powerful Elector of Saxony (a man used to
getting his own way) wanted Schütz to be his Kapellmeister at
the court in Dresden: Schütz reluctantly took up the job in
1617, remaining there for the rest of his long life. All the
same, with an annual salary of 400 florins he was well paid
by the standards of the time. In 1619 he produced his first
major work: a setting of the Psalms of David. The influence
of Gabrieli's echo-effect stereo choruses is everywhere
evident in the splendid music of *Psalmen Davids*, nowhere
better than in the exquisite virtuoso voice-writing in the
100th Psalm ('O be joyful in the Lord all ye lands, serve the
Lord with gladness, and come before his presence with a
song' etc. website 10).

In 1625 Schütz was stricken by the death of his wife after
only five years of marriage. He paid another visit to Venice
where he met Monteverdi and heard his new expressive
settings of dramatic texts. This moved him to try his hand at
writing for the stage, but the score of his opera *Dafne* (1627),
celebrating the marriage of his employer's noble daughter,
has been lost, as has all the rest of Schütz's music for the
stage. There is, incidentally, a reason for this apparent
carelessness where stage works are concerned. Whereas
instrumental, domestic vocal and church music tended to be
published and was reused time and time again, theatre pieces
were usually one-off works. Once the show was over, score

Heinrich Ignaz Franz von Biber (1644–1704)

and parts would be put away in a cupboard and forgotten. The expense of having them printed was certainly not worth it, the more so because opera houses were few and far between at this early stage, and scarcely any performances were public in the modern sense of the word.

The troubles and deprivations of the Thirty Years War at this time put music rather low on the Elector's list of priorities, so between 1633 and 1644 Schütz was allowed to spend three periods as visiting Kapellmeister in Copenhagen. He took up his duties for the Elector again in 1645 (he was now sixty, but his request for retirement was turned down), and in his later years produced three rather severe settings of the Passion according to Luke, John and Matthew as well as a flamboyant *Christmas History* (1664). His employer's death in 1656 finally freed Schütz from his chapel duties, but he continued intermittently to compose eloquent and expressive settings of sacred texts until his death in Dresden at the remarkable age of eighty-seven.

Heinrich Ignaz Franz von Biber (1644–1704)

The Bohemian composer and violinist Heinrich Biber spent most of his life working in the court chapel of the Archbishop of Salzburg, from where his fame spread throughout all musical Europe. His reputation then, as now, rested chiefly on his compositions for violin and his apparently peerless performance of them. Sixteen *Mystery Sonatas* he wrote for Salzburg Cathedral depict scenes from the Bible; they also require some pretty unorthodox tuning of the instrument (known as *scordatura*) to create special effects, such as lowering the pitch of the top (E) string. Another set of Eight Sonatas for solo violin with accompaniment (1681) are quite extraordinarily innovative and unprecedentedly demanding to play, sometimes needing the player's left hand to be at the very end of the fingerboard to reach the highest notes. Biber also produced a body of sacred choral music, including a highly vivid and original Requiem, and even a couple of operas, though he never left his post at the court chapel, where in 1684 he was promoted to *Kapellmeister*.

England

William Lawes (1602–1645)
Henry Lawes (1596–1662)

> *"But you alone may truly boast*
> *That not a syllable is lost;*
> *The writer's, and the setter's skill*
> *At once the ravished ears do fill."*
> Edmund Waller, 'To Mr Henry Lawes'

In the first half of the seventeenth century England was still enjoying what was already a largely outmoded musical genre: consort music for viols – a kind of ancestor of the string quartet. Byrd, Gibbons and others had popularised the form along with a musician called John Coperario (his surname was really Cooper but he changed it after a visit to Italy). Coperario taught the two brothers who were to become big stars on the English musical firmament: William and Henry Lawes.

The elder of the two, Henry (1596–1662), came to know the young Prince Charles (who was four years his junior) through their mutual music teacher, and soon found favour at court when Charles became king in 1625. Henry's most famous work, the music to John Milton's masque *Comus* (1634), says much about his sensitive approach to word-setting – and others besides the great Milton, such as Robert Herrick and Edmund Waller, were also keen to employ him to set their verses. Naturally enough Henry lost his position and fell from grace during Cromwell's Protectorate, but was reinstated in 1660 and indeed composed the anthem for King Charles II's coronation later that year.

Henry's brother William, born in 1602, also worked for Charles I in the capacity of 'musician in ordinary for the lutes and voices', and wrote a lot of instrumental and vocal music for use at court and in the London theatres. A highly skilled and original composer of elegant chamber music, he also possessed an enviable gift for writing flowing melodies. This, together with brother Henry's genius for word-setting, was to be a powerful influence on Henry Purcell and other composers of the next generation. A typical example of William Lawes's easy instrumental elegance is his *Royall Consort* : groups of dance pieces arranged by key into suites. One, in D major, contains the endearing short movement Ecco.

When civil war broke out in England in the 1640s, Charles I moved his court to Oxford. William accompanied him, enlisted in the Royalist army, and was given a commission in the King's personal bodyguard, following his master on campaigns up and down the country. In 1645 the

Royalist forces had almost succeeded in driving the rebels away from the besieged city of Chester when the latter turned and charged their pursuers. William was killed by a bullet in the action that followed, 'betrayed thereunto by his own adventurousness'. Summing up the Parliamentarian fundamentalist attitude to government, it was said by subsequent Royalist sympathisers that 'Will Lawes was slain by those whose wills were laws', and among Royalist ranks his death became a symbol of the excesses of the Puritan revolt.

III. The Fashion Spreads: Different Styles for Different Lands

Even though musicians, like diplomats, could travel unusually freely between countries and courts, an educated seventeenth-century listener would have little difficulty in identifying music from Italy, Germany, France or England. Each country had its own characteristic trademarks. But Italy remained the dominant influence: its two musical giants Gabrieli and Monteverdi had sent echoes resounding through churches, courts and theatres in every corner of Europe, changing for ever the face of music.

Development of Dance Suites

Early in this period, before our system of major and minor keys emerged, it was difficult to write an extended piece of music that had enough aural variety to retain the listener's interest. This difficulty was usually overcome in one of two ways. The first was the use of variation form, which often involved taking a popular tune – *Greensleeves* for example – and, after an initial playthrough, subjecting it to successive kinds of variation, such as a fast-running bass line, changes to the rhythm, lots of ornamentation, and so on. Sweelinck's set of variations on *Mein junges Leben hat ein End* mentioned in Chapter II is a good example.

The second way was by writing pairs of dance tunes, the first being a stately pavane (a kind of slow march) followed by a galliard (a faster dance in triple time – **1**-2-3, **1**-2-3 etc.). Eventually these pairs would fuse with other pairs to form suites. The suite form quickly became a mainstay of Baroque music (Bach was to write dozens of them), built upon the basic frame of two pairs of two contrasted dances: allemande (slow) and courante (fast), and sarabande (slow) and gigue (fast). Sometimes extra dances such as gavottes or minuets were added, but almost invariably suites would be based on those four dances in the same sequence.

Major, Minor and Modulation

The system of major and minor keys which emerged at this time replaced an ancient scheme of modes. This had largely restricted musicians to composing within a predetermined scale of notes that risked becoming boring if it went on for too long (hence the efforts at maintaining interest detailed above). The new concept of moving from one key to another (modulation) came as a godsend, since it enabled composers to write more extended pieces that could move from one scale of notes (key) to another and then return, usually quoting the opening theme as a sort of 'here we are again' landmark. You could compare it to walking up a hill and down the other side instead of walking forever on an interminable flat plain. It is one of those ideas that seems so obvious in retrospect and yet took centuries to evolve.

Composers of opera, too, were quick to exploit the

possibilities offered by the new system of key changes, and in solo vocal numbers (arias) they developed a convention of having an opening section in one key followed by a contrasting middle section in another, succeeded in turn by a reprise of the opening material. This is known as *da capo* form, from the Italian for 'back to the beginning'. Handel's 'Lascia ch'io pianga' from his opera *Rinaldo* discussed in Chapter IV is a typical *da capo* aria. In music, just as in all the other arts and sciences, the Baroque was a time of great discovery and development.

Italy: the Land of Song

Francesco Cavalli (1602–1676)

Italy, a land with a natural affinity for song, had taken opera to its heart – nowhere more so than in Venice, where composers were churning out works for the stage at an astonishing rate. Francesco Cavalli started his professional life singing in Monteverdi's choir at St Mark's, Venice. It was while he was later working as organist in the great basilica of SS Giovanni e Paolo that he helped to set up an opera company in a local theatre, and had his own first opera *Le nozze di Teti e di Peleo* ('The Marriage of Teti and Peleo') produced there in 1639.

Cavalli went on to write nearly thirty operas for Venice – impressive by anyone's standards – and his fame spread so widely that he was invited to Paris to write an opera (*Serse*, 1660) to celebrate the marriage of Louis XIV and the Spanish infanta Maria Theresa. It is for the sensuous, lyrical melodies of his operas that he is remembered today: *Ormindo* (1644), *La Calisto* (1651) and several other works have received successful modern revivals in London and elsewhere, largely thanks to the pioneering work of the musicologist and conductor Raymond Leppard.

Giacomo Carissimi (1605–1674)

Carissimi was another important composer of vocal music at this time, though not for the stage but for the church. After becoming *maestro di cappella* in Rome, in 1650 he was appointed director of music at the church of San Marcello. Carissimi was best known for his fine chamber cantatas and oratorios: one of the latter, *Jeptha*, is probably his most frequently performed work today. Its broad, dignified choruses were to have a strong influence on the choral style of the young Handel when he visited Italy. Carissimi interlaced his choruses with impassioned solo sections and recitatives, and his dramatic way with words can be heard to great effect in a vivid Lament upon the execution of Mary, Queen of Scots. Although much of his music was published during his lifetime, many more of his compositions that existed only in manuscript are now lost.

Alessandro Scarlatti (1660–1725)

> *"He makes use of all sorts of dissonance to express the force of the words and afterwards resolves them so well that indeed the most beautiful concords are hardly so sweet and harmonious as his discords."*
>
> François Raguenet, *Parallèl des italiens et des français*
> (translated 1709)

One late-seventeenth-century opera composer towers above the rest. While the genius of the Sicilian-born Alessandro Scarlatti has been somewhat eclipsed by that of his extraordinary son Domenico, in his day he was one of the greatest musical celebrities in Europe. Born in Palermo into a musical family, he was despatched to Rome while still a boy to study, possibly with Carissimi. While he was there his first opera attracted the attention of the exiled Queen Christina of Sweden, who appointed him musical director of her private theatre. More successes followed, and the remainder of Alessandro's working life was spent in an upward spiral of ever more prestigious musical posts in Rome and in Naples – a city which he can firmly claim to have put on the musical map of Europe.

Alessandro Scarlatti was an exceptionally prolific composer in an age of prolific composers, with at least 114 operas and some 500 small-scale chamber cantatas to his credit. His pastoral Christmas cantata *O di Betlemme* ⟨website 12⟩ contains a lovely aria sung by Mary to her newborn son which, with its soothing melodic lilt and sensitive setting of Italian verse, shows Scarlatti to be a great master of vocal style. It is a miniature masterpiece, and a textbook example of that newly evolved musical sandwich the *da capo* aria.

The Violin

Chamber and instrumental music were also in vogue, with the violin in particular enjoying great popularity. This instrument first appeared in the form we would recognise today in Italy in the early sixteenth century, and a hundred years later it was established as one of the supreme instruments, at the very heart of music. By the start of the eighteenth century, remarkable craftsmen in Cremona (northern Italy) were creating the finest violins that ever were made. Other stringed instruments such as cellos, violas and lutes were also manufactured by these master craftsmen but it is now usual to group them together as 'violin makers'. They are of particular interest because string instruments, unlike wind instruments, do not wear out and become unplayable: if they are good to start with they actually increase in value with age.

The Amati family in Cremona were trailblazers and the first acclaimed masters whose reputation was assured when the French court placed an order for a fleet of string instruments to create an orchestra for the king of France. It was in the Amati workshops that Andrea Guarneri (1626–1698) and Antonio Stradivari (1644–1737) learned their trade. It has been estimated that Stradivari made up to 3,000 violins, violas and cellos in his long life, though the exact quantity is uncertain. Hundreds of them are still in use today: the cellist Mstislav Rostropovich is said to have prized an instrument with a long scratch on it, apparently put there by a careless Napoleon Bonaparte when he snatched it away from a player at his court to have a go himself.

It is highly likely that Cremona became the first centre of the revered art of violin making because of the densely wooded forests in the locality. Makers would reputedly spend long periods in search of trees with the even grain they needed for their instruments, knocking on them to check which ones would resonate best. Later in the eighteenth century, violins made at Mittenwald in Bavaria (which is also set in a region of thick woods) possessed an exceptionally strong and sweet tone that makes them still highly prized today, as much in the auction room as on the concert platform.

Sonatas and Concertos: Alessandro Stradella (1639–1682)

Back in the seventeenth century, instrumental music in the home rivalled the popularity of opera in the theatre, and trio sonatas were the order of the day. 'Trio sonata' is actually a confusing misnomer since the line-up did not necessarily involve three players – it was usually two solo instruments, such as violins, supported by cello and harpsichord filling out the bass. Thousands of such pieces were written and performed, and when the accompaniment of harpsichord and cello was enhanced by the addition of a few extra supporting string instruments, then the sonata had made the short journey that transformed it into a concerto.

Just how vague the terminology of the time was may be demonstrated by the Sonata for Eight Strings with Trumpet `website 13` written by Alessandro Stradella in 1682; it is nothing less than a miniature concerto for double string orchestra with the addition of a bright and merry trumpet part between the opposing forces. Stradella, incidentally, while not in the first division of Baroque composers, is worth mentioning for his colourful life. He was of noble birth, and after musical studies in Bologna he set up as a composer in Rome, leading a distinctly rackety life on the side. He got into all sorts of scrapes with the authorities and was eventually forced to flee the city, ending up in Venice as music teacher to the young mistress of Alvise Contarini, a powerful aristocrat. It was not long before Stradella first had his way and then ran away with her, pursued by the angry aristocrat with a bunch of hired ruffians. According to legend the assassins caught up with Stradella in a church in Turin where he was directing one of his works, but the beauty of the music softened their hearts and instead of killing him they warned him to get out of town.

He ended up in Genoa, playing fast and loose this time with a married noblewoman whose outraged brothers had him bumped off by an altogether less musical hit man. Stradella was a highly skilled and extremely prolific composer, famous in his time for his operas and oratorios. One of the latter, *San Giovanni Battista* ('St John the Baptist'), is still occasionally performed, and is also coincidentally the piece which is supposed to have changed the minds of his would-be murderers in Turin.

Germany

Dietrich Buxtehude (c. 1637–1707)

Meanwhile, in Germany the influence of such instrumental composers as Scheidt and Sweelinck still held sway; and the musical landscape had harpsichords and organs in the foreground. One of its most famous virtuosi in the second half of the seventeenth century was Dietrich Buxtehude – actually a native of Denmark (born in Helsingborg, which only later came under Swedish control) but qualifying as an honorary German through having spent almost all the last forty years of his life at the famous Marienkirche in Lübeck. It seems to have been a tradition at the church, incidentally, that the incoming organist should marry the daughter of the outgoing organist, and almost as soon as he got the job Buxtehude did the right thing and married the daughter of his predecessor Franz Tunder. (When years later the eighteen-year-old Handel came to see about the job in 1703, it seems to have been this clause in the contract that put him off, the girl in question being ten years older than the young lion, and no beauty to boot!) There is a persistent legend that as a youth J.S. Bach walked over 200 miles to Lübeck in order to hear Buxtehude play the organ. On the face of it this is perfectly believable, for the old man's virtuosity and powers of improvisation stood head and shoulders above even his most illustrious contemporaries. One typical example, a Prelude and Fugue in D major, has a strong melodic character and lively rhythm that must have been a real ear-opener for the likes of young Bach and Handel. But there are delights throughout the works of this grand old man whose music is too little heard. One of his greatest choral pieces is a cycle of sacred cantatas, *Membra Jesu nostri* `website 14`, in which a kind of restrained rapture is very much the order of the day.

Johann Pachelbel (1653–1706)

Some years younger than Buxtehude, Pachelbel came from Nuremberg, at the other end of the country, and his lyrical approach to melody seems much closer to the southern Italian style than to that of his northern counterparts. He worked as organist at St Stephen's Cathedral in Vienna and in Stuttgart, before returning to his birthplace for the last nine years of his life.

Though remembered today almost solely for one work, the famous Canon, Pachelbel was a prolific and tuneful composer, as exemplified by a short Toccata in C major `website 15`. Coming from the Italian word for 'touch', a toccata was a keyboard piece designed to sound as though it were being made up on the spot, often in free rhythm with fast running notes. It was extrovert music designed to show off the performer's dexterity, and useful for a player to test the strong and weak points of an unfamiliar instrument – in a different church, for example.

France

Jean-Baptiste Lully (1632–1687)

If you were to ask who was the greatest French composer of the seventeenth century, there would be only one possible answer: an Italian called Lully. Giovanni Battista Lulli was the son of a Florentine miller, and his precocious talent did not go unnoticed. At the age of twelve he was discovered by a French courtier, the Chevalier de Guise, who was on the Grand Tour in Italy. Attracted by the boy's lively character as well as his obvious musical talent, the chevalier took him back to Paris where he became a page in the royal household. Jean-Baptiste Lully, as he was now known, was quick to adapt. He learned French, played the violin and guitar exceptionally well, and rapidly acquired the exaggerated airs and graces in vogue at court. It paid off: in time the young Louis XIV, who was six years Lully's junior, grew fond of him and gave him a place in his own private band: Les Vingt-quatre Violons du Roi.

Jean-Baptiste Lully (1632–1687)

**"He merits with good reason the title of
Prince of French Musicians, being regarded
as the inventor of this beautiful and great French music."**

Titon du Tillet, quoted in Mellers's
François Couperin (1950)

The Baroque concept of tragedy, as epitomised by the French *tragédie en musique* does not necessarily tally with our post-Wagnerian perception of full-on misery. There was always a sense that one went to the theatre to be diverted, not depressed, as the contemporary commentator Jean-François Marmontel explained:

'The essence of tragedy requires that the action should not relax, that everything should inspire fear or pity and the danger or misfortune of the chief characters should increase from scene to scene. But the essence of opera requires that its action be only intermittently distressing and terrible; that its passions should have moments of quiet and happiness, like serene intervals on stormy days. It is enough if care is taken that all happens as in nature, that hope succeeds fear, suffering pleasure, pleasure suffering, with the same ease as in the course of life.'

Lully also studied composition and was soon writing ballets for private performance in which he and the King danced side by side. His virtues – not to mention his sycophancy – were well rewarded when in 1661 he was appointed official composer to the King as well as master of music to the entire royal family, at an astronomical salary.

He collaborated with the dramatist Molière, too, in more ballets for the court, and established what was to become the Grand Opéra in Paris: a national opera house where he not only composed the music for more than a dozen operas, including *Alceste* and *Isis*, but was also director and stage manager. His haughty, arrogant temperament must have made him perfectly at home in the autocratic world of the theatre.

Lully made important innovations in Baroque musical forms. Not only did he invent the *tragédie en musique* but the overtures to his stage works were also ground-breaking. They began with a grand and solemn slow introduction with jerky 'dotted' rhythms that were probably designed to grab the attention of his chattering aristocratic audience, before moving on to a faster, fugal section to lead into the action on stage. This convention proved to be extremely flexible and useful: it was to find particular favour with both Bach and Handel in the following century – and there is no higher recommendation than that! Lully ruled French music and the French stage quite unashamedly to his own advantage for some twenty-five years until an unfortunate accident brought about his untimely death. While beating out the rhythm with a heavy stick during a musical performance, he struck himself on the foot and died of gangrene poisoning.

Like him or not (and nobody who had the misfortune to

work under him seems to have had a good word to say about him) Lully was a brilliant composer and master of many genres. His church music is every bit as theatrical as his works for the stage, perhaps nowhere more obviously than in the splendid Benedictus `website 16` from his late years: devotional music for a great occasion.

Marc-Antoine Charpentier (1643–1704)

Marc-Antoine Charpentier was less formal in his approach to composition than Lully and he not only excelled in the field of opera but also worked as *maître de chapelle* to the Dauphin until he lost the job thanks to Lully's jealous opposition. Later in life he was appointed director of music at the beautiful Sainte-Chapelle in Paris, which had been built in the twelfth century by St Louis to house his most precious relic: the Holy Crown of Thorns. Charpentier's approach to church music is always melodically attractive and appealing to the ear, as in his popular arrangement for voices and organ of *Un Flambeau, Janette, Isabelle!* ('Bring a Torch, Janette, Isabella!' `website 17`), a Christmas carol which is still well known in England.

French Keyboard Music

Instrumentally speaking, French composers were relatively slow to catch up with the easy elegance of sunlit Italian melody, and they never really got to grips with the learned, intellectual patterns of sound being woven in churches beyond the Rhine. Instead, they developed in quite a different direction, partly imitating the arpeggio-like playing of the

French lutenists – known as *style brisé* or 'broken style'.
Harpsichord music tended towards the courtly and formal,
but often had a grave and noble beauty that has won it a lot
of adherents among musicians today.

Jacques Champion de Chambonnières (1601/2–1672)

The founding father of the French school of *clavecinistes*
(harpsichordists) was Jacques Champion de Chambonnières.
He was the son of a musician at the French court, who in turn
became harpsichordist first to Louis XIII and then to his son,
the infant king Louis XIV. Chambonnières wrote more than
140 pieces for harpsichord which he put together into more
than two dozen suites of dances filled with lively courantes
and stately pavanes. One distinguishing (and charming)
feature of French keyboard music is a fondness for giving the
pieces whimsical and often obscure titles: *La Rare* ('The
Beautiful Girl') and *L'Entretien des Dieux* ('The Meeting of
the Gods') are two of Chambonnières's loveliest dance
movements.

Chambonnières must also have excelled as a teacher,
since the two most significant *clavecinistes* of the next
generation both studied under him: Jean Henri d'Anglebert
and Louis Couperin. D'Anglebert (1635–1691) had a rather
more academic approach to keyboard writing than his
contemporaries: his sonorous chaconnes (slow dances in
triple time) have a solid grandeur all their own. But
D'Anglebert did also publish some delightful harpsichord
arrangements of Lully's airs and dances, perhaps at the
suggestion of his patron Louis XIV (D'Anglebert having

succeeded his former teacher Chambonnières as *claveciniste* to
His Majesty).

Louis Couperin (c. 1626–1661)

With Louis Couperin we meet the founding father of a musical
dynasty that flourished in one narrow little tied cottage in the
Marais district of Paris for 200 years, from the middle of the
seventeenth century. Hailing originally from Chaumes, to the
east of the capital (where Brie cheese is made), Couperin arrived
in Paris as a young man to study with Chambonnières, and in
1653 he became organist at the church of St Gervais. The house
that went with the job was tucked away into a corner of the
church wall and can still be seen today in the Rue François
Miron (just a few doors down from the building where the child
Mozart was to stay on his first visit to the French capital).

Louis Couperin seems to have led an uneventful, if short,
life, living with his two brothers, Charles (who would become
father of the most famous Couperin) and François. But his
keyboard music is anything but uneventful; rather it is often
elusive and even mystical – both to hear and to decipher on the
page, since very unusually there are no bar lines to break up the
music into beats. Melodies and, above all, harmonies are there
– but not readily apparent, left for both performer and listener to
assemble in their heads, as it were.

One short work of Louis Couperin's stands alone with a
pathetic sadness. It is a tombeau: a lamenting tribute rather like
a musical funeral. *Le Tombeau de M. de Blancrocher* is a sad
and eloquent expression of love for a dear friend who had fallen
downstairs drunk and presumably broken his neck. M. de

Blancrocher was a celebrated lutenist in his time, and was mourned quite beautifully in this sombre and thoughtful threnody.

England

Henry Purcell (1659–1695)

Until well into the second half of the twentieth century the music of Britain had few advocates on the continent of Europe. The Germans spoke witheringly of 'Das Land ohne Musik', while the French could never find it more than 'tel quel'. But accepting this is to overlook an important exception. Abroad, as well as in his native land, Henry Purcell has long been recognised as one of the most versatile, imaginative, skilled and profound composers in the history of music. The facts of his short life are straightforward enough, if sparse: the son of a musician employed at the court of King Charles II, Purcell was born in Dean's Yard, Westminster (next door to the eponymous Abbey) in 1659. At the age of nine or ten he became a chorister in the Chapel Royal.

Purcell seems likely to have had lessons in composition from the organist of Westminster Abbey, appropriately named John Blow, who was also the composer of one of England's earliest operas, *Venus and Adonis* (c. 1685). By the age of twenty Purcell had succeeded Blow as organist at the Abbey (he had already been the organ's official tuner for four years, at an annual fee of £2). At this time he was beginning to compose incidental music for the stage and was also writing a collection of fantasias for viols.

Henry Purcell (1659–1695)

"In one way Purcell is a finer stage composer than Wagner;
his music is full of movement, of dance.
His is the easiest music in all the world to act."

Gustav Holst, *The Heritage of Music* (1928)

Now that he was settled into his new position at Westminster Abbey, Purcell began to give more attention to writing church music, in which some of his most heart-searching and also sublimely happy music is to be found. Around the time of his marriage in 1681, he composed a short anthem, *Hear My Prayer, O Lord* website 18 , which is a profoundly moving statement of faith composed with a perfect understanding of the wide range of expressive sound that a full choir can produce. Even today, its anguished dissonances still sound strikingly modern and are an instantly recognisable trademark of Purcell's style.

> *"Musick is the exaltation of poetry. Both of them may excel apart, but surely they are most excellent when they are joyn'd, because nothing is then wanting to either of their proportions; for thus they appear like wit and beauty in the same person."*
>
> Henry Purcell, Preface to *Dioclesian*, 1690

In 1683 came the first of his Odes for St Cecilia's Day (the patron saint of music), along with an increased quantity of music for the theatre. His score for the semi-opera *Dioclesian* (1690) seems to have brought him to the attention of the poet John Dryden, resulting in a collaboration that produced the sumptuous score for the latter's *King Arthur* the following year, featuring a famous shivering scene of 'frozen' music. Incidental music for *The Fairy Queen*, a rewrite of Shakespeare's *A Midsummer Night's Dream*, also appeared at this time, with Purcell clearly revelling in the bawdy humour of the original.

By this time Purcell had already written his operatic masterpiece: *Dido and Aeneas.* Unlikely as it may seem, it was apparently composed for Mr Josias Priest's boarding school for young gentlewomen in Chelsea. At any rate it was certainly performed there in 1689. The story is taken from Book Four of Virgil's *Aeneid*, in which the hero Aeneas, returning from Troy, is shipwrecked at Carthage where he falls in love with its queen, Dido. But the gods urge him to leave and the broken-hearted Dido kills herself. The final aria of this short opera is known as 'Dido's Lament' website 19 , in which the distraught heroine sings of her approaching death:

> When I am laid in earth
> May my wrongs create
> No trouble in thy breast;
> Remember me, but ah! forget my fate.

Sung over a slow, descending ground bass of only ten notes, the aria is one of the most intensely moving pieces in all English music. It transforms the doggerel of the song's words into real poetry, and lingers in the mind long after the music has ceased.

A few years later, at the end of the freezing winter of 1695, the Abbey choir was singing Purcell's Funeral Music for Queen Mary, another tragic outpouring of loneliness and misery. Worse was to come: before the year was out they would sing that music again, this time at Purcell's own funeral. It is a pathetic footnote to the story of a great man to add that he reportedly died from taking cold after being locked out of his own house in Westminster and forced to spend all night on the doorstep by a wife who was

Thomas Killigrew was one of the leading figures on London's theatre scene once theatres reopened after the Civil War. In 1660 he and Sir William Davenant were granted a patent which allowed them to form two companies under the patronage of the King (Charles II) and the Duke of York. These two companies went on to monopolise the London theatre scene and, as Samuel Pepys noted in his diary in 1667, Killigrew was eager to boast of his success:

'That the stage is now by his pains a thousand times better and more glorious than ever heretofore. Now, wax-candles, and many of them; then, not above 3lb. of tallow. Now, all things civil, no rudeness anywhere; then, as in a bear-garden. Then, two or three fiddlers; now, nine or ten of the best. Then, nothing but rushes upon the ground and everything else mean; and now, all otherwise. Then, the Queen seldom and the King would never come; now, not the King only for state, but all civil people do think they may come as well as any.'

exasperated at the amount of time her husband spent with his friends in the local tavern. At what Purcell would have achieved with another thirty years of creative life before him, we are left to guess.

IV. Full Flower: High Baroque

As the eighteenth century dawned, thanks to affordable printing and the creative genius of the previous generation of musicians, composers had at their fingertips a greater range of stylistic possibilities than ever before. Germans knew French and Italian styles almost as well as their own, and Italian composers were even learning to write fugues and add more colours to their palette. The process of cross-fertilisation was complete. Bach and Handel were to be the shining examples here, absorbing all the new sounds available and reinventing them to create music that was magically different, utterly international, and as potent now as it was then. England, apart from being home to Handel, played virtually no part in this unprecedented miracle, but for one important exception: thanks to already having experienced a democratic (and bloodless) revolution, it became the venue for some of Europe's first public concerts and concert halls. London's opera houses functioned more or less independently of aristocratic patronage, its theatres equipped with first-class orchestras plus an international swarm of bad-tempered divas and star castrati.

In fact, soon after 1700, Baroque music seems to have fused into a dazzling homogeneous delight of satisfying harmony and counterpoint, of achievements that may have been equalled but have never been surpassed. Musically speaking, the Baroque era came to an end in the middle of the eighteenth century with the biggest cultural volcanic explosion that had ever been witnessed.

Italy

The Concerto Grosso

One of the most important musical forms to emerge in the Baroque era was the concerto, in which one (or, less commonly, two or three) instruments are pitted against an orchestra. As the eighteenth century drew near, audiences in Italy began to hear a new form of orchestral music in their churches, theatres and salons: the concerto grosso. Quite simply this was a short work in three or four movements that contrasted a small group of instruments against the main body of players. The most important name linked to the birth of the new music was Arcangelo Corelli, 'il divino' as he was known.

Arcangelo Corelli (1653–1713)

For such a famous and successful musician, Corelli wrote remarkably little, merely four sets of trio sonatas, one of solo violin sonatas and twelve concerti grossi (Op. 6). The concertos contain much ravishing music, and the eighth one (known as the 'Christmas Concerto' website 28 because of the instruction 'written for the night before Christmas' at the top of

Arcangelo Corelli (1653–1713)

"I never met with any man that suffered his passions to hurry him away so much whilst he was playing on the violin as the famous Arcangelo Corelli, whose eyes will sometimes turn as red as fire."

François Raguenet, *Parallèl des italiens et des français*
(translated 1709)

the score) has become a perennial favourite, particularly the Pastorale with which the piece ends.

Born near Bologna, Corelli began to learn the violin as a child, and went on to become one of the greatest virtuosi of the age. In his teens he moved to Rome, which remained his home virtually for the rest of his life. Reports of his playing travelled far and wide, and aspiring violinists flocked to Rome for lessons from 'the true Orpheus'. His tone was of an exceptional sweetness, it was agreed, if marred by the way he sometimes rolled his eyes violently and grimaced while performing. Physically he was small, while his manner was modest and unassuming, though he was admired for his conversational abilities. Musically he was a phenomenon, revolutionising the art of bowing in Italian orchestras and being one of the first systematically to play chords on the violin – a difficult feat. After his death, Corelli was honoured by being buried near Raphael in the Pantheon, and he left a fine and valuable collection of pictures – including works by Bruegel and Poussin – to his patron Cardinal Pietro Ottoboni.

Antonio Vivaldi (1678–1741)

Today, Corelli's concertos have been largely eclipsed by those of the Venetian musician and priest Antonio Vivaldi. If it is a case of strength in numbers then Vivaldi wins hands down, with around 500 to his name. Most familiar of course are *The Four Seasons*, concertos that follow us into lifts, hotel lobbies, shopping centres, restaurants, and even telephone lines as 'hold' music. Red-headed like his violinist father (hence his nickname 'Red Priest'), Vivaldi was also a chronic asthmatic,

Antonio Vivaldi (1678–1741)

"Vivaldi... has a prodigious fury for composition.
I heard him undertake to compose a concerto, with all the parts,
with greater dispatch than a copyist can copy it."

Charles de Brosses, Letter (1739)

though this does not seem to have interfered with his prodigious output as a composer.

He studied the violin with his father, who worked in St Mark's, Venice, and he entered the priesthood at the age of fifteen, taking Holy Orders ten years later. In the same year, 1703, he was appointed violin teacher at one of Venice's most important musical centres, a music school for orphaned girls called the Conservatorio dell' Ospedale della Pietà. Though its great days of seagoing power were by then in decline, Venice was still a cultural focal point of Europe, a place where musical education was taken extremely seriously. Concerts at the Pietà attracted large audiences, especially of foreign travellers who had heard tales of the famous girls' choir and orchestra.

One exceptionally attractive set of Vivaldi's concertos is a group of six, Op. 10, for solo flute and strings. In No. 3 in D, called 'Il gardellino' ('The goldfinch' website 21), solo violins help the flute to mimic the song of the little bird – just one example of Vivaldi's brilliant programmatic writing.

It must have been the public thirst for novelty and pressure from his employers that turned Vivaldi into such a prolific composer: new works were expected for every feast day at the Pietà, and in Italy they have more than most! He once boasted that he could compose a concerto faster than a copyist could write out the parts, and is said to have completed the score of one of his many operas, *Tito Manlio*, in just five days.

Vivaldi's church music also features prominently in concert programmes today; his two best-known choral works, a *Beatus vir* and a vibrant setting of the Gloria, were more complex and altogether on a larger scale than anything he

An account of a visit to the Pietà in Venice, in 1739, by Charles de Brosses:

'Among them [the ospedali] the Pietà is probably the largest; in it about 900 girls, all foundlings apart from those from poor families who are admitted as boarders, receive food and lodging. These children, who, however, are not all foundlings but are sometimes the legitimate offspring of needy parents who are too poor to raise them themselves and therefore secretly place them at night time in the stone cavity on the wall of the hospital, are educated in the above-mentioned manner, and it is a matter for wonder that many excel not only in vocal music but also in instrumental music playing the violin, cello, organ, theorbo and even the oboe and recorder in masterly fashion. Especially renowned are the singers Apollonia and Geltruda, the organist Tonina, the theorbist Prudenza, the oboist Susanna and the violinist Anna Maria, of whom, on this very difficult and delicate instrument, few virtuosos of our sex are the equals.'

wrote for the girls of the Pietà. Each is virtually half an hour in duration. The setting of *Beatus vir* ('Blessed is the man' (website 22 ▶)) is the more elaborate of the two: composed for double orchestra and choir, it is a wonderfully uplifting work, as ebullient as anything he ever wrote for the opera house.

It seems as if Vivaldi became restless after several years at the Pietà, for much of his later life was spent abroad. He travelled in 1725 to Amsterdam, the city in which his music was published (in fact only a small quantity of it was published either during his life or for a hundred years afterwards: the cult of Vivaldi is a relatively modern one). Though they never met, Bach was a confessed admirer of Vivaldi's concertos and transcribed six of them for solo keyboard.

In 1741 Vivaldi went to Vienna, where the Emperor Charles VI had earlier made him welcome; but he died of an unidentified stomach ailment just a month after he arrived. Today his music is more popular than ever before, and for good reason, charged as it is with graceful melody, infectious virtuosity and an irresistible rhythmic energy.

Baroque Concertos beyond Vivaldi

Beyond Corelli and Vivaldi, of course, there were dozens of lesser Italian orchestral and chamber composers whose names have been lost in the mists of time and, in the middle, a handful of men whose music is still played to the great enjoyment of modern listeners. Tomaso Albinoni (1671–1751) is one such case, a wealthy Venetian and amateur composer who had no need to earn his living (he described himself as a dilettante) but was nevertheless a distinguished violinist and composer of fifty operas. Ironically, though, he was not responsible for the *Adagio* which is now the most famous work attached to his name, for that is a twentieth-century fake! Bach was fond of Albinoni's music and arranged sections from his trio sonatas for keyboard.

Two gifted Venetians were the Marcello brothers, Alessandro (1669–1747) and Benedetto (1686–1739), both of whom wrote church and instrumental music of great lyrical beauty. A famous oboe concerto in D minor, usually ascribed to Benedetto though it may actually be the work of his brother, is still popular in the concert hall today.

The Tuscan Francesco Geminiani (1687–1762), born in Lucca, is another interesting figure. A pupil both of Corelli in Rome and Alessandro Scarlatti in Naples, he emigrated first to London and then to Dublin where he established a concert hall. He was much in demand for his virtuoso skill on the violin and for his lively, tuneful compositions which include about forty concerti grossi modelled on those of Corelli. He made a lot of money but seems to have been something of a shiftless character, spending time in a debtor's prison; an unsuccessful sideline as an art dealer may have been responsible for his trouble in this respect.

Last of all in this gallery of instrumental virtuosi comes Giuseppe Tartini (1692–1770), though he only just qualifies as a Baroque musician, dying in the year that Beethoven was born. He came from a wealthy Florentine family and seemed set for a life of luxury, but got into trouble while a student at Padua University when he concealed his priesthood status and married a young girl he was teaching. He was forced to leave the university (and his bride) in something of a hurry, and took shelter in the Franciscan monastery at Assisi. The work for which he is best remembered today, the 'Devil's Trill' Sonata, is supposed to have been written there, after the Devil appeared to Tartini in a dream, playing the violin. (The fiendish trill, incidentally, occurs in the last movement.) Tartini used to give concerts concealed behind a curtain in the monastery but, although his identity was eventually uncovered, charges against him were dropped and he was reunited with his wife. He became revered as one of the most cultured musicians of his day, playing throughout Italy to huge audiences and publishing numerous sets of violin concertos and sonatas. His last years were spent in Padua, where he founded an important music conservatory in 1728.

Domenico Scarlatti (1685–1757)

The next major Italian to appear on the scene is one of the greatest of all. He was the most extraordinary virtuoso the harpsichord has ever seen, the composer of hundreds of exotically brilliant sonatas for the instrument (some 570 are currently known). He could have had all Europe at his feet, yet Domenico Scarlatti chose to hide himself away in the remote royal courts of Portugal and Spain. Considering the scant knowledge we have of his life, it is as if the man deliberately set out to obliterate all traces of himself.

The son of the great Neapolitan composer Alessandro Scarlatti, Domenico – along with Handel and J.S. Bach – is one of three master musicians born in the *annus mirabilis* of Baroque music, 1685. The facts of his life are certainly few.

Domenico Scarlatti (1685–1757)

"It is time to consider how Domenico Scarlatti condensed so much music into so few bars with never a crabbed turn or congested cadence, never a boast or a see-here."

Basil Bunting, *Briggflatts* (1966)

He learned music from his father, and by the age of eighteen had already had two operas produced in Naples. A year later he went to Venice for lessons from the famous theorist Francesco Gasparini.

By 1709 he was in Rome, where he became *maestro di cappella* to the exiled Queen Maria Casimira of Poland and wrote operas that were performed in her private theatre there. It was at this time that a fabled musical duel with Handel is said to have taken place, in which the young Saxon was given the laurels for playing the organ while Scarlatti was adjudged master on the harpsichord. At any rate, the two respected and admired each other: years later Handel was to quote some of Scarlatti's harpsichord sonatas in his Op. 6 concerti grossi.

Scarlatti worked at the Vatican for a while, and in 1720 had an opera produced at the Haymarket Theatre in London (though there is no evidence that he ever visited England). There is in fact only one, tantalising, glimpse of Scarlatti at the keyboard, reported from Italy by a young Irish musician called Thomas Roseingrave, who describes seeing 'a grave young man in black and with a black wig' at a reception, who sat down at the harpsichord 'and when he played it was as if ten hundred devils had been at the instrument'; Roseingrave 'had never heard such passages of execution and effect before'.

The next sighting of Scarlatti is in Lisbon, where he had become *maestro di cappella* to Maria Barbara of Braganza, Princess of the Asturias. He was to remain in her service for the rest of his life. In 1729, when Maria Barbara married the heir to the Spanish throne, Scarlatti accompanied her to

Madrid, and spent his remaining years following the royal court on its relentless seasonal progress from Madrid down to Seville and up to the oppressive confines of the Escorial. And all the time he was still composing countless one-movement sonatas for harpsichord. He died in Madrid in 1757 aged seventy-one, shortly after completing a ravishing setting of the *Salve regina* for soprano and strings.

A few collections of Scarlatti's sonatas were published during his lifetime, chiefly in London and perhaps through his connections with Handel or Roseingrave. What we do have is a collection of hundreds of neatly copied manuscripts of his pieces in sumptuously bound volumes that belonged to the queen of Spain, who must have been a magnificent player if she could cope with the astounding difficulty that is one of the hallmarks of this astonishing music.

The well-known Sonata in E major, K. 380 **website 25** is one of Scarlatti's more slowly paced pieces. This *Andante* is a royal procession complete with trumpets and drums, and beautifully conceived in terms of the harpsichord. This piece, like his other popular works in the repertory today, is often played on a modern piano and sounds quite at home; what is lost in acidic bite is compensated for by the piano's greater dynamic possibilities.

By contrast, Sonata K. 96 in D major **website 24** is much more rapid, containing lightning hand-crossings which demand incredible agility from the player. It recalls another courtly occasion, this time a hunt. Opening with horn-like fanfares, the music shifts to mimic the flashing hooves of the horses galloping and taking breakneck leaps over hedges and ditches, only breaking off in the second half inexplicably to burst out into what sounds like a fit of giggles! Scarlatti added the words 'Viva felice!' ('Live happily!') to one of his published collections, which is something like what happens when listening to this music.

Germany

Johann Sebastian Bach (1685–1750)

The classic *Baker's Biographical Dictionary of Musicians* is quite clear about Bach's stature: 'Supreme arbiter and lawgiver of music, a master comparable in stature with Aristotle in philosophy and Leonardo da Vinci in art,' and few who know anything about his work would take issue with that. Quite simply the most accomplished musician who ever lived, Bach had complete and utter control over every aspect of his prodigious art. By the time he was born at Eisenach in the German province of Thuringia on 21 March 1685, the Bachs had already been musicians for some generations: he himself was to have four professional musicians among his twenty children, and the line continued well into the nineteenth century.

The story of his life, however, is hardly an epic saga in itself. Orphaned while still a child, he was largely brought up by an elder brother, and after attending the local school in the town where his brother lived he went on to complete his education in the prosperous north German town of Lüneburg as a chorister in the Michaeliskirche. At the age of eighteen he became organist in the little town of Arnstadt, from where he journeyed in 1705 to hear Buxtehude in

Johann Sebastian Bach (1685–1750)

"Bach is a colossus of Rhodes, beneath whom all musicians pass and will continue to pass. Mozart is the most beautiful, Rossini the most brilliant, but Bach is the most comprehensive: he has said all there is to say."

Charles Gounod, in *Le Figaro* (1891)

Lübeck – though it is unlikely that he travelled the whole distance (a round trip of more than 200 miles) on foot, as legend has it.

On his return, he became organist at the Blasiuskirche in Mühlhausen in 1707, and in the same year married his cousin Maria Barbara Bach. An upbeat G major Prelude and Fugue `website 25`, BWV 550 for organ with a massive pedal solo, probably dates from this period in the composer's life.

Though he appears to have been comfortable enough in Mühlhausen, Bach abandoned the job the following year in favour of a post as court organist to Duke Wilhelm Ernst of Weimar, and it was here that he wrote the bulk of his enormous output for organ. After eight years he wanted to move on, but this was hardly the era of employee rights and Wilhelm Ernst was having none of it, refusing to let him leave; as a result Bach ended up spending November 1717 in prison for insubordination. After a month, however, he was released and summarily dismissed from his job. Six of his children were born while he was at Weimar, including Carl Philipp Emanuel (to whom the illustrious Telemann was godfather). Bach had also written a fine body of music there, but there is little doubt that he would have been heartily glad to shake the Weimar dust from his shoes.

His next post, where he remained for six years until May 1723, was as Kapellmeister and court director of music to Prince Leopold of Anhalt-Cöthen. This job came with special responsibility for the Prince's orchestra: devotional music was not required of him and the salary was almost half as much again as he had earned in his last position. Small wonder that his work there began very happily: Prince Leopold was a keen musician who played both the violin and the harpsichord, and was a good singer too. For much of the time, to judge by his output, Bach was in a white heat of compositional activity. Most of his set of six concerti grossi, the Brandenburg Concertos website 26 , date from this time. They were not originally planned as a set but were simply 'concertos for several instruments'. And what concertos! From the virtuoso trumpet writing in the Second Concerto to the weirdly dark (violin-less) scoring of the Sixth, via the extraordinary Fifth (effectively the first keyboard concerto ever written), these works never cease to scintillate and thrill, no matter how often you hear them.

At least two of Bach's four Orchestral Suites (Nos 1 and 4) seem to have been composed at Cöthen, but in these busy years he was primarily occupied with instrumental music for smaller groups or soloists. The six solo Cello Suites, six Violin Sonatas and Partitas (also unaccompanied), and sonatas for violin and harpsichord and for flute and harpsichord are only a fraction of Bach's achievements during his fertile period here.

While working for Prince Leopold, Bach was also extremely busy as a teacher, his wife and children being among his many pupils. Much of the harpsichord music that dates from this time – the first five of the six French Suites, the six enigmatically titled English Suites, the two- and three-part Inventions – may have originated from the need to develop the hands and minds of those he taught.

Book I of *The Well-Tempered Clavier* (which contains twenty-four preludes and fugues – one in each major and minor key) also dates from these years. The idea behind it was to promote a system of tuning known as equal temperament, in which for the first time the octave would be divided into twelve equal semitones so that a keyboard instrument would always sound in tune in whichever key it was being played. The system is now used for pianos and other keyboard instruments all over the world. Both the preludes and fugues vary widely in mood and form: in the hands of such a genius counterpoint is not a confining way of writing music, for fugal form can be one of the freest of all. This is brilliantly demonstrated in the fugue of the G minor Prelude and Fugue (website 27) from Book 1 of *The Well-Tempered Clavier.*

One vocal work to emerge from Bach's secular years at the Prince's court was the so-called 'Wedding' Cantata, *Weichet nur, betrübte Schatten* (website 28), BWV 202, intended to add to the merrymaking at the wedding feast. It begins in an introverted mood, and towards the end there is a short aria for soprano that is as happy and tender as anything Bach ever wrote. It also offers a superb example of its composer's genius for combining melodies simultaneously.

It was on his return from a visit to Karlsbad with Prince Leopold in 1720 that Bach discovered his beloved wife had fallen ill and died during his absence. In all likelihood this shattering experience led to his application for the post of organist in Hamburg. He was offered it, though in the event he turned it down.

In 1721 he married his second wife Anna Magdalena, a gifted singer six years his junior. She was to bear him another thirteen children. Later in 1721 another wedding took place when Prince Leopold married his cousin Federica, who intruded

Martin Heinrich Fuhrmann, clearly a well-travelled gentleman, gave this vivid eyewitness account of Bach's keyboard playing in 1729:

'When I was at the Easter Fair in Leipzig recently… I had the good fortune to hear the world-famous Mr Bach. I thought the Italian Frescobaldi had polished off the art of keyboard playing all by himself, and Carissimi was a most valued and cherished organist. But if I were to put the two Italians with their art on one side of the scales and the German Bach on the other, the latter would far outweigh them, and they would be lifted straight up into the air.'

upon her husband's friendly relations with his court composer enough to confirm Bach's decision to withdraw from Cöthen.

His next move was to be his last. Johann Kuhnau, the elderly Cantor of the Thomasschule in Leipzig, had recently died. Leipzig was a big city with a population of around 30,000 and a fine university. It had long been a centre of publishing, and the post was an important one. The city elders had chosen Bach's friend Telemann for the job, but after the council in Hamburg where Telemann worked refused to let him go, and after months of wrangling, the Leipzig authorities finally offered the job to Bach, who arrived in the spring of 1723 to take up his duties.

The job was certainly no sinecure: in addition to organising the music for all services in the city's two principal churches, he had to teach the choristers for upwards of twenty hours per week – and that included Latin lessons as well as music and singing. He was also responsible for the boys' discipline, and had to take prayers and supervise school meals. All of which amounted to rather more than a forty-hour week, so Bach was eventually forced to pay a lower-ranking teacher out of his own pocket to take over his non-musical duties, which made a substantial hole in his annual salary. As if this were not enough, he soon found out that the civic authorities were narrow-minded and reactionary in the extreme, and his relationship with them, which was rarely less than prickly, would sometimes flare up into serious argument. One famous instance of this concerned Bach's practice of accompanying the Lutheran hymns with decorated parts for his hands and feet at the organ (as in one of his most famous pieces, 'Jesu, joy of man's desiring'): it led the city worthies to complain that they never knew when to start singing!

But in spite of his onerous workload and less than happy circumstances, it was while Cantor in Leipzig that Bach composed his greatest sacred music: the *Christmas Oratorio*, the *St Matthew Passion* and the *St John Passion*. In addition to this, a cantata was performed at every main Sunday service and Bach wrote almost 300 of these (of which about one third are now lost). Orchestral players to accompany the cantatas were drawn from the Thomasschule, from amateur musicians in the city or from the university music society, the Collegium Musicum, whose director was Bach himself.

Composing one cantata per month on average for more than twenty-five years, in addition to carrying out his other duties, musical and non-musical, is a feat that would beggar belief if the evidence were not there. The sheer variety of raw emotion, vivid tone-painting, technical genius and profound musical beauty is there for all to hear: as a creative accomplishment the cantatas defy comparison with anything else in the history of music. But most important of all are Bach's settings of the Passion story: these are among his greatest inspirations. Two of them survive complete, though there is evidence to show that he wrote others. The *St Matthew Passion*, BWV 244 (website 29) dates from either 1727 or 1729 and is a highly charged drama: the Evangelist supplies the linking narrative, while the roles of Jesus and lesser characters such as Pilate and the apostle Peter are contrasted with a chorus representing the crowd. The moment when the crowd shouts for the criminal Barabbas to be released is as exhilarating as it is chilling, while the grief-stricken chorus that ends the work 'Wir setzen uns mit Tränen nieder' ('In Tears of Grief') is almost operatic in character.

There were consolations in Bach's difficult time at Leipzig, however – not least the concerts and conviviality to be found in the Collegium Musicum which met at a local coffee house on Friday evenings. Bach produced a series of harpsichord concertos, mostly arrangements, to be played there. The slow movement of the Keyboard Concerto in F minor, BWV 1056 website 38 is unique in being scored for virtually a solo melodic line against *pizzicato* strings. Though short, it has a starry eloquence that brings with it a glimpse of eternity: you want it to go on for ever.

Towards the end of the seventeenth century Bach's predecessor in Leipzig, Kuhnau, had published a collection of harpsichord suites which he called *Clavier Übung* (Keyboard Exercise), and when Bach came to publish volumes of his own harpsichord music the same title seemed ideal for the job. Volume I consisted of six large-scale suites that he called partitas. These consisted of the customary four movements as explained in Chapter III (allemande, courante, sarabande, gigue) interspersed with extra dances and preceded by a substantial prelude. They are among his most frequently performed works in the keyboard repertory today.

The final part of the *Clavier Übung* is technically the most demanding music he ever wrote for the keyboard. Bach's is not the ostentatious kind of music that calls for the performer to throw himself from the top to the bottom of the keyboard and back again in the twinkling of an eye (like Scarlatti's, for instance): instead it demands complete independence and equality of each of the fingers, so that the hands may convincingly carry four separate lines of music as clearly and evenly as if each were played by a separate instrument. The so-called Goldberg Variations consist of a highly ornamented but fundamentally simple little sarabande (here called 'Aria') with thirty variations, though the variations are not on the melody at all but on the bass line. They are complicated in form and awesomely demanding to play, yet the listener is only aware of a sublime sense of satisfaction.

Much of the music of Bach's later years became ever more deeply involved with the intricacies of counterpoint. *The Musical Offering* (which contains a formidable six-part fugue on a gawky, misshapen theme given to him by King Frederick the Great) and *The Art of Fugue* both date from the final years of Bach's life – in fact the latter, a collection of fugues on a single theme, breaks off in the middle when the composer's failing sight no longer permitted him to carry on. After a brief period of blindness he died of a cerebral haemorrhage on 28 July 1750.

Bach's ability to absorb all the different styles of music available in Europe and synthesise them into a coherent whole makes him the keystone of almost everything that came after him. His name and his music may have been unfamiliar to the general public for nearly 100 years after his death, until the young Mendelssohn revived the *St Matthew Passion*; but Haydn, Mozart and Beethoven all studied and revered the technical, emotional and spiritual perfection of music's greatest musician.

German Opera

In the early eighteenth century the capacity of German composers for assimilating foreign styles into their own music led to the first great flowering of opera there, the start of a love affair that was to continue right down the centuries and into our own time. It was centred in the north German city of Hamburg which, as the country's chief port and former headquarters of the mighty Hanseatic League, was also its most cosmopolitan commercial centre. Three composers led the way out of the church and into the theatre, and even though little of this music is now to be heard outside its native land, the birth of a national school of operatic composition marked a turning point in Germany's cultural life.

Reinhard Keiser (1674–1739)

The eldest of these three key figures was the son of an organist. Reinhard Keiser attended the Thomasschule in Leipzig as a boy, thirty years before Bach arrived there. Before the age of twenty he was already writing pastiche operas for the theatre in Brunswick, and by 1696 he had become chorus-master of the Hamburg Opera, rising to co-director while still in his twenties. He handled a busy schedule, producing not just his own works but also operas by such key figures as Handel, Telemann and Johann Mattheson. He seems to have written well over 100 operas of various types, predominantly on classical themes but also in the German language – a big plus as far as the paying public was concerned. Hopefully it is only a temporary misfortune that the man once called 'the father of German melody' should be largely neglected today.

Johann Mattheson (1681–1764)

The second major player in Hamburg's brief Golden Age of music was a diplomat, lexicographer, linguist and legal eagle as well as a composer. Johann Mattheson started out as a child prodigy; by the age of nine he could play several instruments and was organist of more than one Hamburg church, while moonlighting in the chorus of the Hamburg Opera. Soon afterwards, having mastered English, Italian and French, he was studying law as well as singing solo roles in the opera house.

In 1703 he met and befriended Handel, but the two of them were soon to have a famous quarrel that almost ended in catastrophe. In 1704 Handel directed from the harpsichord a performance of Mattheson's latest opera, *Cleopatra*, in Hamburg, with the composer on stage singing the lead tenor role. On leaving the stage when his scene was over, Mattheson asked Handel to let him take over at the keyboard – the opera being his very own, after all. When Handel refused a row broke out, resulting in a duel. Handel's life was saved, so the story goes, when Mattheson's thrusting sword snapped off on a metal button of Handel's coat. Whatever the truth of the matter, the pair were soon fast friends again. Handel later left the city and Mattheson, ever the master multi-tasker, went on to become director of music at Hamburg Cathedral, while at the same time pursuing employment as private secretary to the British envoy in the city.

Georg Philipp Telemann (1681–1767)

The most prominent and prolific musician of his time and the third of the trio to set German opera on the road to greatness

Johann Mattheson (1681–1764)

was Georg Philipp Telemann, the son of a clergyman in Magdeburg, Saxony. He learned violin, harpsichord, flute, zither and organ while still a boy and like his exact contemporary Mattheson was sent off to university to read law. But music intervened, and he abandoned his legal studies for a succession of ever more significant musical appointments, eventually becoming civic music director in Hamburg as well as director of the Hamburg Opera.

He became a firm friend of Bach and Handel and seems to have been loved by all who knew him – apart from his wife, who ran off with an officer in the Swedish army.

Telemann wrote more than twenty operas each for Leipzig and for Hamburg as well as a staggering quantity of orchestral, chamber and instrumental music before his long working life was finally curtailed by a crippling eye disease. Some orchestral suites he wrote for the Darmstadt court, and known as the 'Darmstadt Overtures' (even though each so-called 'Overture' comprises several short movements beginning with an overture!), are among the most attractive works in his output (as witnessed by the website's movement from his Overture in D Major, TWV 55: D15

website 31 .

Telemann has sometimes been accused of superficiality, but although his music is certainly approachable, the accusation is unjustified. He had a fine mastery of every known form of composition, and 'could write a motet in eight parts as easily as another could write a letter,' according to Handel. Through his study and understanding of the French composers, especially Lully, he introduced a new note of grace and gaiety to German music.

Georg Philipp Telemann (1681–1767)

**"If there is nothing new to be found in melody
then we must seek novelty in harmony."**

Georg Phillipp Telemann, Letter (1751)

Letter of 1723 from Telemann to Johann Friedrich Armand von Uffenbach, town councillor at Frankfurt who had supported the composer's musical activities during his time there:

'Although music slides downhill at Frankfurt, here it climbs steadily; and I believe that nowhere can one find a place where the mind and spirit of the musician is more stimulated than at Hamburg. One great factor in this is that as well as the many nobility here, the city fathers and indeed the whole town council attend the public concerts; they are attracted by the sensible judgement of so many connoisseurs and clever people. Then too there is the opera, now in the fullest flower; and finally that *nervus rerum gerendarum* [money] which can hardly be said to be glued fast to the music-lovers here.'

France

In France the omnipotent and overbearing Lully proved a hard act to follow, but musically speaking the first half of the eighteenth century was dominated by two figures, one of them a church composer (François Couperin) and the other a man of the theatre (Jean-Philippe Rameau). Today, however, they are valued equally for their keyboard music: both published enormously popular books of harpsichord suites that have remained in the repertory, while Couperin's sacred vocal music and even Rameau's operas now lie outside the choral and operatic mainstream.

François Couperin (1668–1733)

Known as 'Le Grand' to distinguish him from less important members of this great musical family, François Couperin was the nephew of the keyboard composer Louis Couperin (mentioned earlier, p. 50–1) and among the five generations of family musicians to inhabit the organist's house attached to the church of St Gervais in Paris. Though he held the church position from 1685 until his death, he was also organist at the Royal Chapel and harpsichordist to the King, which necessitated a three-month residence at Versailles each year. But Couperin moved easily in society and was music master to many members of the royal family, including the Dauphin. On his death, incidentally, his daughter Marguérite-Antoinette became the first-ever woman to be appointed harpsichordist to the French King.

Couperin was a prolific composer of harpsichord music, publishing twenty-seven *ordres* (suites) in four volumes during

François Couperin (1668–1733)

**"The Italian style and the French style have for long divided
the Republic of Music in France. For my part, I have always
valued those works which have merit, without regard for their
composer or country of origin."**

François Couperin, Les Goûts réunis (1724)

his lifetime. Some of them contain up to twenty pieces, though on the composer's own admission players were not necessarily expected to perform these suites complete. Nearly all are given fanciful titles, often a reference to some character in Couperin's own circle of acquaintance. Most are decorated by elaborate trills and other ornaments which heighten the music's sensibilities: unlike the piano, however hard you strike the keys of a harpsichord the music gets no louder, so the ornaments are used to provide different stresses and accents to important notes (see panel opposite).

A tenderly expressive slow movement from his *Premier Ordre* entitled 'Les Sentiments' website 32 is a good example of the ornaments helping to give both shape and pace to the music. Further on in the same suite, a faster musical miniature he enigmatically called 'La Manon' website 33 shows how the ornaments can lend a sophistication and subtlety to some otherwise routine and workaday keyboard conventions.

In 1716, at the height of his fame and success, Couperin published a manual on harpsichord playing, *L'Art de toucher le clavecin*, which was widely acclaimed and even familiar to Bach hundreds of miles away in small-town Germany. For harpsichordists today it contains invaluable guidance on performing the music of the period – with such delightful details as how to sit at a harpsichord wearing a light smile for the assembled company.

> *"I declare in all good faith that I am more pleased with what moves me than with what astonishes me."*
> François Couperin, *L'Art de toucher le clavecin (1716)*

François Couperin, in the introduction to Volume Four of his harpsichord suites, is clearly not best pleased at the cavalier approach taken by too many performers:

'After taking such care to mark the ornaments suitable for my pieces, I am always surprised to hear of those who have learned them with no heed to my instructions. This is unpardonable negligence, the more so as it is no arbitrary matter to put in any ornament that one may wish. I declare, therefore, that my pieces must be executed as I have marked them, and that they will never make an impression on those persons of real taste unless one observes to the letter all that I have marked without any additions or deletions.'

Jean-Philippe Rameau (1683–1764)

Couperin was not the only French composer to write an important manual. Rameau wrote a highly influential treatise on harmony in which he presented music as a science, though you would never guess that from hearing his music. Of all the performers and composers who filled the courts of eighteenth-century France, Rameau was the only musician who achieved the same level of supremacy in society as Couperin. The son of a provincial organist in Dijon, Rameau as a boy studied music there with the Jesuits. Following a short stay in Italy, he was installed as organist of Notre Dame in Avignon and eventually settled in Paris. Rameau's burning ambition was to write music for the stage, and successes soon began to mount up. Works such as *Hippolyte et Aricie* (1733), *Les Indes galantes* (1735) and *Castor et Pollux* (1737) brought him both fame and money, and are well represented in record catalogues today. Performances, however, are relatively uncommon outside France, for his operas work best when treated to lavish and costly productions.

But even if the plot and action of these gilded Baroque showpieces seem mannered to a public weaned on the *verismo* of Puccini and the dark sparkle of Verdi, French Baroque opera has red blood in its veins and sometimes a high pulse rate too. Since the time of Lully, ballet had played a large part in these extravaganzas, and the dance music Rameau wrote for his own operas is one of their most appealing features today. *Les Boréades* website 34 , his last work, has a particularly convoluted storyline involving Boreas (the North Wind of the title), a *deus ex machina* descending from the heavens, and the Fifth Cavalry storming to the rescue

Jean-Philippe Rameau (1683–1764)

"In music the ear obeys only nature. It takes account of neither measure nor range. Instinct alone leads it."

Jean-Philippe Rameau,
Observations sur notre instinct pour la musique (1734)

in the form of the god Apollo. All pretty far-fetched to today's audiences perhaps, but the incidental dances in it are as fresh now as they ever were. The orchestration in particular is nothing short of brilliant in comparison with the clumsy efforts at writing for orchestras in the opera house elsewhere in Europe at the time. Only Handel could have come close. The opera was never produced in Rameau's lifetime, unfortunately, as the eighty-three-year-old composer succumbed to typhoid fever during rehearsals; it had to wait until the twentieth century to be staged.

Rameau was a complex character, an intellectual and a friend of Voltaire whose enlightened views he largely shared. As a composer he stands between the declining Baroque style and the new, simpler elegance of the later eighteenth century. His feeling for melody, rich harmony and innovative instrumentation in orchestral music makes his style immediately recognisable and places him among the finest composers of the age.

His harpsichord music, too, is highly original and vivid, and in places calls for an extremely skilled technique. But it can also be beguilingly simple. Two of his best-known short pieces for the instrument come from his E minor suite: a 'Musette' website 35 (French for a bagpipe, and used here to indicate the drone effect in the bass) which conjures up perfectly those stiflingly hot summer afternoons in the French countryside when only the bees have the energy to move at all; and a short peasant dance called 'Tambourin' website 36, in which the sophisticated theorist throws his learning to the winds to recreate the music of a band of cheerful rustics.

During the Baroque era, the debate between national styles raged, nowhere more so than between French and Italian styles. Here are two opposing views of the rights and wrongs of Rameau's style:

'It is to M. Rameau that we owe this mongrel kind which passes to-day in France for Italian music; a veritable flickering; no agreement of the tune with the words nor of the airs with the situations of the characters… Am I fated to hear nothing but this foreign, hateful, baroque, inhuman music?'

'M. Rameau is impugned for what deserves our admiration… His music is neither purely French nor purely Italian. It has the graces and gentleness of the one without its monotony; the depth and genius of the other without reeking of learning.'

England

Following the premature death of Purcell in 1695, composition in England was in something of a slump. Opera was predominantly an imported Italian commodity, instrumental music came in the form of imported virtuoso wizards with printed material from the continental mainland, and most orchestral music was also imported. But, while having next to nothing home-grown on the shelves, London was an unrivalled importer of music and musicians and probably the leading cosmopolitan cultural centre in the world. Then, early on in the eighteenth century, a visitor arrived in London who would change its musical face forever.

George Frideric Handel (1685–1759)

Georg Friedrich Händel (as he was originally called) began life on 23 February 1685, the son of a barber-surgeon in Halle, Saxony. The father also doubled as gentleman's gentleman to a local princeling, the Duke of Saxe-Weissenfels. This duke was sharp enough to notice a nascent talent in his valet's son and had the boy sent for music lessons to the Kapellmeister at Halle's principal church, Friedrich Zachau. Here, Handel was taught organ, harpsichord and the rudiments of composition.

At the age of seventeen he matriculated at Halle University and became organist at the local cathedral. But he rejected the career of church musician that his father had planned for him and, in 1703, took himself off to Hamburg, which had recently become the centre of German opera. In charge there he found Reinhard Keiser and Johann Mattheson,

George Frideric Handel (1685–1759)

**"Handel understands effect better than any of us –
when he chooses, he strikes like a thunderbolt."**

Wolfgang Amadeus Mozart,
quoted in Percy M. Young, *Handel* (1947)

with whom he readily fell in (though he would fall out, notoriously, with the latter). He stayed in Hamburg for almost three years and had his first opera (*Almira*) produced there while still in his teens.

In 1706 Handel left for Italy, the focal point of opera in Europe, and visited Florence, Rome, Naples and Venice. In these cities he had operas and other works performed, quickly attracting the attention of influential patrons as being something out of the ordinary. A chance meeting in Venice with the Elector of Hanover's Master of Horse brought his Italian sojourn to an end: in 1710 he returned to Germany as the Elector's Kapellmeister. Almost immediately he sought and was granted permission to visit England, where he overstayed his leave disgracefully but enjoyed a huge success with his opera *Rinaldo*, which had fifteen performances at the Queen's Theatre in London during the winter season of 1710–11. One aria from this story of the Crusades, 'Lascia ch'io pianga' ('Leave Me to Weep' website 37), was a particular hit at the time, and its heart-rending air of pathos has continued to move audiences ever since.

Back in Hanover the following summer (1711) he almost immediately requested leave for another English trip, which was reluctantly granted with the proviso that he 'return within a reasonable time'. More operas followed when he was back in London, as well as an Ode for Queen Anne's Birthday performed at Windsor Castle in 1713 and a grand *Te Deum* to celebrate the Peace of Utrecht later that same year. By now, of course, Handel had seriously overstayed his leave of absence.

The young composer was mortified when Queen Anne died early the following year. He had still not returned to his job in Hanover when, as luck would have it, his boss the Elector became King George I of England. For a while even the insolent Handel lacked the cheek to show his face at court, but the rift was healed and all forgiven (legend has it that this came about through a surprise alfresco performance of the so-called 'Water Music' while the King and Queen were being rowed up the Thames). Whatever the circumstances, King George showed himself to be a generous man, granting Handel an annual stipend of £400.

In 1717, in addition to writing operas for the London theatres, Handel went to work for the Duke of Chandos at Cannons, his splendid country house in Middlesex, north of London. Here he wrote a magnificent set of anthems for his employer, now known as the 'Chandos Anthems'. He also reworked an earlier piece written for performance in Italy: *Acis and Galatea*, to a libretto by John Gay. This was produced at Cannons in 1718. It tells the usual shepherd-meets-shepherdess story, with the difference that the shepherd Acis is killed by a rock thrown by the jealous one-eyed Cyclops Polyphemus, and transformed, in the manner of classical mythology, into a limpid stream. Polyphemus's lustful song 'O ruddier than the cherry' website 38 quickly became a drawing-room standard and is still a favourite with basses today, a magically conceived aria in this pastoral mini-tragedy.

Italian opera was all the rage, and a group of wealthy backers drawn from high society clubbed together to form a company that engaged composers and singers to stage it. Named the Royal Academy of Music (and not to be confused with the venerable teaching institution), the company was most active between 1720 and 1728, its two chief composers

The performance of Handel's 'Water Music', as reported in *The Daily Courant* on July 19, 1717:

'On Wednesday Evening [17 July 1717], at about 8, the King took water at Whitehall in an open Barge, wherein were also the Dutchess of Bolton, the Dutchess of Newcastle, the Countess of Godolphin, Madam Kilmanseck, and the Earl of Orkney. All went up the River towards Chelsea. Many other Barges with Persons of Quality attended, and so great a Number of Boats, that the whole River in a manner was cover'd; a City Company's Barge was employ'd for the Musick, wherein were 50 Instruments of all sorts, who play'd all the Way from Lambeth (while the Barges drove with the Tide without Rowing, as far as Chelsea) the finest Symphonies, compos'd express for this Occasion, by Mr Hendel; which his Majesty liked so well, that he caus'd it to be plaid over three times in going and returning. At Eleven his Majesty went a-shore at Chelsea, where a Supper was prepar'd, and then there was another very fine Consort of Musick, which lasted till 2; after which, his Majesty came again into his Barge, and return'd the same Way, the Musick continuing to play till he landed.'

being Handel and an elder Italian contemporary of his, Giovanni Bononcini (1670–1747). There was no love lost between the two. Their rivalry hit the headlines with monotonous regularity until Bononcini was finally disgraced by accusations of plagiarism and further murky tales involving alchemy and other doubtful occupations. Poor old Bononcini fled abroad and worked as a freelance musician on the Continent before dying in obscurity in Vienna with a meagre pension granted him by the Empress Maria Theresa.

Those years saw the composition of some of Handel's finest operas: *Giulio Cesare, Rodelinda, Scipione* – about twelve in all, and all with ancient classical subjects. But by 1728 the public was getting a little tired of all this Italian fare and the Academy's funds were foundering. Handel took over the business himself in 1729 but it soon became evident that the jaded palates of London wanted something fresh. In one respect the English did have something fresh in 1727 – a new king, George II, for whose coronation in Westminster Abbey Handel wrote the well-loved anthem *Zadok the Priest*. He was now a naturalised Englishman himself, having signed the documents and sworn the oath the previous year.

Although Handel considered himself a man of the theatre, the stage was by no means his exclusive concern, even during the busiest decades of his life. He was a superb organist and harpsichordist, as a book of eight suites for the latter instrument published in London in 1720 testifies. The fifth of the set contains the well-known air and variations 'The Harmonious Blacksmith', while the seventh suite in G minor ends with a rumbustious and grandiloquent

Passacaglia ⟨websit2 39⟩ which is actually a set of variations on a straightforward sequence of eight chords. There is much to show that Handel was at his best as an improviser at the keyboard: it is our bad luck that he wrote so little down.

As the public wearied of temperamental divas and castrati on stage, Handel (ever the shrewd businessman) had something new ready for them. These were sacred dramas: oratorios. They were less expensive to mount than opera and perfectly suited to an English middle-class audience which was socially excluded from the costly seats and expensive fashions in the opera house. Oratorios also cleverly exploited one aspect of English musical life that had survived the onslaught of imported foreign music since the death of Purcell: its great choral tradition, of which the British have always been justly proud. Sung in English by English singers, these oratorios could hardly fail.

And they didn't. To begin with, oratorio was an extremely dramatic art form. As a rule these works were given in theatres rather than churches and some of Handel's libretti actually contain stage directions – a clear indication that the composer would have liked oratorios to have been acted, though this does not appear to have happened. All of them apart from *Theodora* (his own favourite) and *Messiah* are based on Old Testament stories, and in between acts Handel would often play an organ concerto, a feature of the performances that audiences loved. He had first hit upon the idea of oratorio years before, but not on this scale: in the 1730s and 1740s he produced some two dozen masterpieces in the form, including *Saul*, *Athalia* (first performed at the Sheldonian Theatre in Oxford), *Israel in Egypt*, *Judas Maccabeus* and, of course, *Messiah*.

Messiah, although far and away the most popular of the great string of English oratorios, is unusual. Not directly dramatic, it is more akin to the German versions of the Passion story in that it relies upon commentary rather than character to tell its story (i.e. there is no acting, and the singers are not in costume). Beginning with Old Testament prophecies, it traces the life of Christ from birth through to death and resurrection. It was written for performance in Dublin, taking less than a month to complete and being rehearsed with a scratch group of singers in Chester where the composer stopped on his way to catch the packet boat to Ireland.

Its Dublin premiere on 13 April 1742 was a triumph: the public was awestruck by the vivid word-painting that is such a feature of its massive choruses. The cries of joy that follow one another in 'For unto us a child is born' website 40 may be familiar fare to all of us now, but imagine the effect of those stamping chords on the people who first heard the work. It was not so well received the following year in London, even though King George stood up at the end of the 'Hallelujah' Chorus, if the story is to be believed; but *Messiah* soon entered the souls of its English listeners, who took it into their hearts in their own way and have been humming and whistling it ever since.

Apart from writing oratorios, Handel appears to have occupied himself almost entirely by performing and composing other genres of music. In the course of a single month, October 1739, he sat down and produced his Twelve Grand Concertos, Op. 6. Written for strings with keyboard continuo, and in the meatier movements pitching a small solo group against the rest of the band, they hark back to Corelli's concerti grossi. They are written in the Baroque suite form; yet at the same time some parts of these wonderful works seem to anticipate the symphony.

Early on in the set, Handel quotes unashamedly from a book of harpsichord sonatas recently published in London by his old friend Domenico Scarlatti. A darker element pervades the later concertos; but even here there are flashes of sunlight, such as a miniature gavotte with variations, from his Concerto grosso in D minor (website 41), that could almost have come from the pen of Haydn or one of his contemporaries a generation later. Melody is what matters in this little piece: the snippets of eighteenth-century ornamentation around it already seem like old-fashioned decorations that are going to be thrown away after the party.

Handel surely sensed that the musical world was changing around him – for years he had been at its very centre – and a different world was coming to the fore. But he soldiered on, the grand old man of the theatre who still sat unchallenged on the throne of English music. In later life he was plagued by eye trouble and was effectively blinded by the same incompetent quack who had earlier destroyed the sight of J.S. Bach. Handel went with increasing frequency to stay with his aristocratic friends at their country houses where he was ever a welcome bachelor guest, and kept up a wide correspondence: to his friend Telemann, a keen gardener, he despatched at least one box of plants from England.

Handel died in the spring of 1759 at his house in London, leaving a fortune of £20,000 (the bulk of which was bequeathed to a niece in Germany). He was buried with due pomp and circumstance in Westminster Abbey, where

Roubiliac's fine sculpture of him may still be seen. The whole of England mourned, knowing that it would never see his like again.

Handel's English Contemporaries

If not totally eclipsed by his long shadow, Handel's contemporaries in England were very much a reserve team, though they included some interesting figures.

Thomas Augustine Arne (1710–1778)

Arne was a younger contemporary of Handel, and also a man of the theatre. Though his music is tender, cheerful and of real melodic charm, he himself seems to have been something of a truculent sourpuss. He was born a stone's throw away from Covent Garden market, the son of an upholsterer who must have been exceptionally successful, as he sent young Thomas to Eton. From there, Arne was put into a solicitor's office, but secretly concentrated instead on developing his gifts on the harpsichord and violin. His father's anger on finding out eventually softened, and the young man had his first opera *Rosamond* produced in London (with his brother and sister both appearing in it) when he was twenty-three.

Other operas, masques and incidental music followed: one of them, a historical masque called *Alfred* first performed at the country house of Cliveden (then a residence of the Prince of Wales), contains what must be Arne's most famous song: 'Rule, Britannia'. Although his selfish and quarrelsome nature made him enemies wherever he went, his music was hugely popular. Arne's settings of Shakespeare songs, notably

Thomas Augustine Arne (1710–1778)

"It is probable that not a notion of duty ever occurred to Dr Arne, so happy was his self-complacency in the fertility of his invention and the ease of his compositions, and so dazzled by the brilliancy of his success in his powers of melody – which, in truth, for the English stage, were in sweetness and variety unrivalled."

Fanny Burney, quoted in Langley's *Doctor Arne* (1938)

those in *As You Like It* and 'Where the Bee Sucks' from *The Tempest*, have remained in the repertory ever since they were written, thanks to the freshness that is characteristic of all his work.

Charles Avison (1709–1770)

Orchestral concertos with and without soloists were central to the music of mid-eighteenth-century England, possibly thanks to the huge success of Handel's Op. 6 set. One of the most popular providers of these was Charles Avison, who appears to have studied in London with Geminiani before returning to his native Newcastle as organist. He set up a series of subscription concerts that were among the earliest public concerts in the country. His many concertos for strings have enjoyed something of a renaissance over the last twenty years. Avison's music is light and airy in texture, with a warmth and spontaneity that makes this renewed interest entirely understandable.

William Boyce (1711–1779)

Boyce, in contrast, was an altogether weightier musician than Avison, and one of the few English musicians of his time to bear comparison with his counterparts on the Continent. As a boy he was a chorister at St Paul's before studying the organ and eventually being appointed Master of the King's Musick. He was also very active in the theatre, collaborating with the actor–manager David Garrick on a number of projects. Boyce was unusual among his contemporaries in taking a keen interest in the music of the past. He collected anthems, services and other church music from as early as the reign of Henry VIII 200 years before and right up to his own time, including works by Byrd, Tye, Tallis and John Bull, names that were quite forgotten outside the confines of English cathedrals.

In his orchestral concertos, engaging though they are, Boyce finds it hard to avoid the shadow of the great Handel, whose music he admired to the point of adoration. However, Boyce was probably the first English composer to write symphonies – fairly four-square and naive symphonies maybe, but symphonies nonetheless. By the time of his death the age of the Baroque was gone forever and musical dominance was already passing from Italy to Austria.

Coda

The writing had been on the wall for some years, truth to tell. The impact of Handel and other leading composers – particularly of opera – in Italy, in addition to the vast flow of chamber and instrumental music in the now rather formal 'old style', had mined the marvellous seam of Baroque music to exhaustion. Audiences and composers alike turned from the elaborate conventions of Baroque music to look for something simpler, more personal and direct.

By the time Handel died in 1759 Haydn, the happy harbinger of the Classical age, was twenty-seven and embarking on his first serious career move; the *wunderkind* Mozart was three years old and already starting to compose; while in Germany C.P.E. Bach and his brothers were opening the window to let the fugue out. Within the next generation such masterpieces as Mozart's *Marriage of Figaro*, Beethoven's *Fidelio* and Haydn's oratorio *The Seasons* were to celebrate and deal with real people instead of pasteboard figures from classical mythology. No longer was music the exclusive concern of princely courts and overfed archbishops: the middle classes were here to stay, and they wanted their own music. In fewer than a hundred years there would be a piano in every household.

Sources of Featured Panels

Page 16: Coryat, Thomas, 'Coryat's Crudities; hastily gobled up in five moneths travels' (London, 1611); in Piero Weiss and Richard Taruskin, eds, *Music in the Western World: A History in Documents*, Schirmer, 1984

Page 20: Arnold, Denis, *The Master Musicians: Monteverdi*, J.M. Dent, 1962

Page 46: Girdlestone, Cuthbert, *Jean-Philippe Rameau: His Life and Work*, Cassell, 1957

Page 55: Westrup, J.A., *The Master Musicians: Purcell*, J.M. Dent, 1965

Page 63: Talbot, Michael, *The Sacred Vocal Music of Antonio Vivaldi*, Leo S. Olschki Editore, 1995

Page 75: David, Hans T. and Mendel, Arthur, eds, *The New Bach Reader*, rev. Christoph Wolff, W.W. Norton, 1998

Page 85: Petzoldt, Richard, *Georg Philipp Telemann*, trans. Horace Fitzpatrick, Ernest Benn, 1974

Page 89: Anthony, James R., *French Baroque Music*, Batsford, 1978

Page 93: Girdlestone, Cuthbert, *Jean-Philippe Rameau: His Life and Work*, Cassell, 1957

Page 98: Burrows, Donald, *The Master Musicians: Handel*, Schirmer, 1994

A Timeline of the Baroque Era

	Music	History
1600	Peri and Caccini *Euridice* (Florence); Cavalieri *Rappresentatione di anima et di corpo* (Rome)	Giordano Bruno burned by the Inquisition in Rome for heresy; British East India Company formed
1601	Monteverdi becomes *maestro di cappella* at Mantua	
1602	Cavalieri dies; Cavalli born	Dutch East India Company formed
1603	Artusi criticises Monteverdi's style	Elizabeth I of England dies; Champlain explores St Lawrence river
1604	Dowland *Lachrimae or Seaven Teares*	
1605	Monteverdi publishes Fifth Book of madrigals, with reply to Artusi's criticisms	
1606		

Art and Architecture	Literature
Claude Lorrain born; Caravaggio and Annibale Carracci working in Rome	Donne *Songs and Sonnets*
Rubens employed at Mantua for seven years, travels extensively in Italy and Spain	Shakespeare *Hamlet*; idem, *Twelfth Night*
Domenichino moves to Rome	
	Shakespeare *Othello*
	Cervantes *Don Quixote* (first part); Bacon *The Advancement of Learning*
Rembrandt born; Caravaggio *The Seven Works of Mercy*	Corneille born; Shakespeare *Macbeth*; Ben Jonson *Volpone*

	Music	History
1607	Monteverdi *Orfeo*	English colony of Virginia founded
1608	Frescobaldi becomes organist of St Peter's, Rome; Monteverdi *Arianna* (lost)	Protestant Union formed in Germany
1609	Schütz goes to study in Venice with Giovanni Gabrieli	Kepler publishes his first two laws of planetary motion
1610	Monteverdi *Vespers of the Blessed Virgin*; Cima *Concerti ecclesiastici*, including first known sonata for violin and continuo	Henri IV of France assassinated, succeeded by Louis XIII; Galileo observes moons of Jupiter
1611		Turks invade Hungary
1612	Giovanni Gabrieli dies; Praetorius *Terpsichore*	
1613	Monteverdi takes up post at St Mark's, Venice	
1614	Banchieri founds Accademia dei Floridi (Bologna)	Dutch found colony of New Amsterdam, later New York
1615	Schütz 'borrowed' by Dresden court, then given permanent post	
1616		Galileo promises not to teach Copernican system
1617		

Art and Architecture	Literature
	Milton born
Caravaggio *Beheading of St John the Baptist*	
Rubens first employed as court painter in Brussels	Shakespeare *Sonnets* first published
Caravaggio dies	
Rubens begins *The Descent from the Cross*	English Bible, Authorised Version; Shakespeare *The Tempest*
	Giovanni Battista Guarini dies (author of *Il pastor fido*)
El Greco dies	
Inigo Jones appointed surveyor of the King's works, England	Cervantes *Don Quixote* (second part)
	Shakespeare dies; Cervantes dies
Murillo born	

	Music	History
1618	Caccini dies; Praetorius *Syntagma Musicum* (parts 2 and 3)	Thirty Years War begins: German states, Holland, Scandinavia and England (Protestant) vs Habsburg Empire and Spain (Catholic)
1619	Schütz *Psalmen Davids*	
1620		Pilgrim Fathers land at Plymouth, Massachusetts
1621	Sweelinck dies; Praetorius dies	
1622		
1623	Byrd dies	
1624		England and Spain at war
1625	Gibbons dies; Schütz *Cantiones sacrae*	Charles I becomes king of England
1626	Dowland dies; Legrenzi born; Louis XIII establishes Les Vingt-quatre Violons du Roi	
1627	Schütz *Dafne* (lost), the first German opera	siege of Huguenots at La Rochelle by Cardinal Richelieu

Art and Architecture	Literature
	Sir Walter Raleigh executed
Nicholas Hilliard dies; Banqueting House, Whitehall begun (Inigo Jones)	
	Bacon *Novum Organum*
	La Fontaine born
	Molière born
Maffeo Barberini installed as Pope Urban VIII; employs Bernini to help fulfil grand project to glorify Rome; Velásquez appointed court painter, Madrid	Pascal born; Shakespeare First Folio published
Hals *Laughing Cavalier*; Bernini begins colossal bronze baldacchino for St Peter's, Rome	
Poussin settles in Rome under patronage of Cardinal Barberini	
	Bacon dies

	Music	History
1628		Huguenots surrender and forfeit political rights
1629	Schütz *Symphoniae sacrae*	Charles I dissolves English parliament
1630		
1631		
1632	Lully born; Monteverdi *Scherzi musicali*	Gustavus Adolphus of Sweden wins victory for Protestant powers at Lutzen
1633	Peri dies	Galileo summoned to Rome, forced to recant his theories
1634	Banchieri dies; Henry Lawes provides music for Milton's mask *Comus*	
1635	Frescobaldi *Fiori musicali*	
1636	Marin Mersenne *Harmonie universelle*	
1637	Buxtehude born; first public opera house opens in Venice	

Art and Architecture	Literature
Ruisdael born; Pietro da Cortona begins altarpiece *The Trinity* for St Peter's, Rome	John Bunyan born
Rubens *Allegory of Peace*; Bernini becomes principal architect of St Peter's	
Velásquez travels in Italy; Rubens knighted by Charles I of England	
Rembrandt moves to Amsterdam	Donne dies; Dryden born
Vermeer born; Wren born; Van Dyck appointed portrait painter to Charles I of England; Rembrandt *The Anatomy Lesson of Doctor Tulp*	John Locke born; Spinoza born
S. Carlo alle Quattro Fontane, Rome begun (Borromini); Mauritshuis, The Hague begun (Jacob van Campen)	
Luca Giordano born; Rubens completes cycle of paintings for ceiling of Banqueting Hall in Whitehall	Milton *Comus*
Rembrandt *The Feast of Belshazzar*	Cardinal Richelieu founds the Académie Française
	Nicholas Boileau born; Corneille *Le Cid*
	Descartes *Discourse on Method*

Music	History
1638 Monteverdi *Madrigali guerrieri et amorosi*	
1639	
1640 Monteverdi *Il ritorno d'Ulisse in patria*	Portugal wins independence from Spain
1641	
1642 Monteverdi *L'incoronazione di Poppea*	Newton born; beginning of Civil War in England; French found Montreal; Louis XIV (aged five) succeeds to French throne
1643 Charpentier born; Frescobaldi dies; Monteverdi dies	
1644 Antonio Stradivari born (Cremona); Barbara Strozzi first book of madrigals	
1645 William Lawes dies	
1646 Cavalli's *Egisto* performed at Palais Royal, Paris	

Art and Architecture	Literature
Hobbema born; Poussin *Israelites Gathering Manna*	
Rubens's last version of *The Judgement of Paris*; Pietro da Cortona finishes ceiling fresco *Allegory of Divine Providence* for Barberini Palace, Rome	Racine born
Rubens dies	Descartes *Meditations on First Philosophy*
Palais Royal built, Paris; Domenichino dies; Van Dyck dies	
Rembrandt *The Night Watch*	
Bernini begins work on Cornaro chapel in S. Maria della Vittoria, Rome, combining architecture, sculpture and painting to create strong dramatic effect	

Music	History
1647 Pelham Humfrey born	
1648 Schütz *Geistliche Chor-Musik*	Treaty of Westphalia ends Thirty Years War
1649 John Blow born	Charles I of England beheaded
1650 Athanasius Kircher *Musurgia universalis* (a compendium of musical facts and theories)	
1651 Playford *English Dancing Master*	end of Civil War in England
1652	Dutch found colony at Cape of Good Hope
1653 Corelli born; Pachelbel born; Lully is appointed composer at French court; Froberger court organist at Vienna	Oliver Cromwell becomes Lord Protector of England
1654 Scheidt dies	
1655	Sweden declares war on Poland
1656 Queen Christina of Sweden resident in Rome, with Carissimi as *maestro di cappella*	Swedish victory at Warsaw: hostilities follow vs Russia, Denmark and Holy Roman Empire
1657	

Art and Architecture	Literature

Velásquez makes second visit to Italy

Velásquez *The Toilet of Venus*   Descartes dies

Hobbes *Leviathan*

Georges de La Tour dies

Rembrandt *Aristotle Contemplating the Bust of Homer*

Rembrandt *Bathsheba*

Velásquez *Las Meninas*; Bernini re-engaged by new pope for work at St Peter's, Rome, and makes plans for a square in front with colonnade

	Music	History
1658		
1659	Purcell born; Christopher Simpson *The Division-Violist*	Treaty of the Pyrenees guarantees French supremacy over Spain
1660	Alessandro Scarlatti born; Hamburg Collegium Musicum founded	Restoration of monarchy in England; first meeting of an embryonic Royal Society, London
1661	Louis Couperin dies; Lully becomes *surintendant de la musique de la chambre* at French court	
1662		Boyle's Law formulated
1663		Turks begin to advance through the Balkans
1664	Lully's first collaboration with Molière	
1665		
1666	Accademia Filarmonica founded, Bologna	Great Fire of London; Christiaan Huygens appointed president of the Académie des Sciences by Louis XIV
1667	Froberger dies	

Art and Architecture	Literature
Velásquez appointed to highest order of Spanish knighthood	
Velásquez dies; Murillo *Birth of the Virgin*, for Seville cathedral	Daniel Defoe born; Pepys begins to write his diary
Charles Le Brun decorates Galerie d'Apollon, the Louvre; work begins at Louis XIV's Versailles to transform it into the grandest palace in Europe	
Le Brun 'first painter to the King'	Pascal dies
Le Brun becomes director both of Gobelins factory and the Académie Royale; grand staircase to Vatican, Rome (Bernini)	
	Molière *Tartuffe*
Poussin dies	La Fontaine *Tales and News in Verse*
Hals dies; Rembrandt *The Suicide of Lucretia*	Molière *Le Misanthrope*
	Swift born; Milton *Paradise Lost*; Racine *Andromaque*

	Music	History
1668	François Couperin born; Buxtehude organist at Marienkirche, Lübeck; Blow organist at Westminster Abbey, London	triple alliance of England, Sweden and Netherlands vs France
1669	Pierre Perrin and Robert Cambert granted a patent to present operas in French	Venice cedes part of Crete to Turks
1670		
1671	Albinoni born; Académie d'Opéra, under Perrin and Cambert, performs a pastorale	Turks declare war on Poland; Leibniz begins work on a calculating machine
1672	Schütz dies; Lully gains monopoly of all opera in France; first concerts in London charging admission for entry	
1673		
1674	Carissimi dies; Lully *Alceste*	
1675	Lully *Thésée*	Royal Observatory founded, Greenwich
1676	Cavalli dies; Thomas Mace *Musick's Monument*	Turkey gains Polish Ukraine
1677	Matthew Locke dies	

Art and Architecture	Literature
S. Lorenzo, Turin begun (Guarino Guarini)	La Fontaine *Selected Fables*
Rembrandt dies; Pietro da Cortona dies	
	Pascal *Pensées* published
	Molière dies
Vermeer dies; rebuilding of St Paul's cathedral, London begun (Wren)	Philipp Spener *Pia desideria*, an inspiration for the Pietist movement in Germany
Hôtel des Invalides, Paris completed (Liberal Bruant)	Spinoza dies; Racine *Phèdre*

	Music	History
1678	Vivaldi born	René de la Salle explores Great Lakes
1679	Zelenka born; Purcell succeeds Blow as organist at Westminster Abbey, London; A. Scarlatti's first opera, Rome	Edmond Halley publishes map of stars of the southern hemisphere
1680		
1681	Mattheson born; Telemann born; Corelli publishes Trio Sonatas, Op. 1 (Rome)	William Penn given charter to found Pennsylvania in North America
1682		
1683	Rameau born; Purcell *Sonnata's of III Parts*	Turks besiege Vienna: at war with Austria to 1699
1684	A. Scarlatti *maestro di cappella* at Naples court; Kuhnau organist at Thomaskirche, Leipzig; Biber Kapellmeister at Salzburg	Holy League formed by Pope vs Turkey; Newton's *Principia* demonstrates law of gravity
1685	Bach born; Handel born; Domenico Scarlatti born; Corelli publishes Sonate da camera, Op. 2 (Rome)	emigration of French Huguenots after Edict of Nantes is revoked; Catholic James II becomes king of England
1686	Playford dies; Nicola Porpora born; Lully *Armide*; Legrenzi *maestro di cappella* at St Mark's, Venice	League of Augsburg formed: Holy Roman Empire, Spain, Sweden etc. vs France

Art and Architecture	Literature
Giovanni Battista Gaulli ceiling fresco *Adoration of the Name of Jesus* for Il Gesù, Rome	Bunyan *The Pilgrim's Progress*
Le Brun decorates Galerie des Glaces, Versailles	Hobbes dies
Bernini dies	La Rochefoucauld dies; Comédie Française founded in Paris
Claude Lorrain dies; Murillo dies; Ruisdael dies	
Watteau born	Corneille dies; Pierre Bayle founds *Nouvelles de la République des Lettres*
François Girardon begins equestrian statue of Louis XIV, Place Vendôme, Paris	
	Fontenelle *La Pluralité des mondes*, a popular compendium of scientific enquiry

	Music	History
1687	Lully dies; Geminiani born; Jean Rousseau *Traité de la viole*	Christian Thomasius the first German academic to lecture in his own language
1688		Glorious Revolution in England: Whig lords invite Protestant William of Orange to invade
1689	Purcell *Dido and Aeneas*; D'Anglebert *Pièces de clavecin*	
1690	Legrenzi dies; Biber ennobled at Imperial Court	Christiaan Huygens describes wave theory of light
1691		
1692	Tartini born; Purcell *The Fairy Queen*	Anglo-Dutch fleet defeats French at La Hogue
1693	Couperin one of four *organistes du Roi* at Versailles	Robert Boyle *General History of the Air* published
1694	Corelli publishes Trio Sonatas, Op. 4 (Rome); Campra *maître de musique* at Nôtre Dame, Paris	
1695	Purcell dies; Locatelli born; Jeremiah Clarke organist at St Paul's, London; Purcell *The Indian Queen*; Muffat *Florilegium primum*	

Art and Architecture	Literature
St Florian monastery, Austria designed (Carlo Antonio Carlone)	Bunyan dies; Pope born
	Montesquieu born
Claudio Coello finishes grand altarpiece *Charles II Adoring the Host* for El Escorial, Madrid	Locke *Essay Concerning Human Understanding*
Andrea Pozzo begins ceiling frescoes for St Ignazio, Rome	Claude Fleury begins *Histoire ecclésiastique* in 20 volumes
Luca Giordano paints ceiling vault of imperial staircase, El Escorial, Madrid	
Schloss Belvedere, Vienna begun (Johann von Hildebrandt)	
Greenwich Hospital, London begun (Wren)	Voltaire born; *Dictionnaire de l'Académie Française*
	La Fontaine dies; Bayle *Dictionnaire historique et critique*

	Music	History
1696	Kuhnau *Sieben Suonaten*, the earliest publication where 'sonata' signifies music for solo instrument	Peter the Great of Russia takes Azov from Turkey
1697	Leclair born; Quantz born; Estienne Roger sets up music printing business, Amsterdam	Treaty of Ryswick: France returns Spanish conquests
1698	Bartolomeo Cristofori begins to build a keyboard instrument producing 'il piano e il forte'	
1699	J.A. Hasse born; Mattheson's first opera performed, Hamburg	Treaty of Karłowitz: Austria takes Hungary from Turkey, Poland takes Turkish Ukraine
1700	Faustina Bordoni born; Corelli publishes Sonatas for violin, Op. 5 (Rome)	war breaks out between Russia and Sweden for control of the Baltic (to 1721)
1701	Kuhnau Cantor of Thomaskirche, Leipzig	War of Spanish Succession begins (to 1714): alliance of England, Netherlands, German states and Empire vs France
1702	Telemann founds Collegium Musicum for students at Leipzig university	
1703	Vivaldi *maestro di violino* at Ospedale della Pietà, Venice; Bach organist at Neukirche, Arnstadt	Peter the Great builds a new capital, St Petersburg

Art and Architecture	Literature
Tiepolo born	
Canaletto born; Hogarth born	Charles Perrault *Contes de ma mère l'oye*
	Pietro Metastasio born
Castle Howard designed (Vanbrugh)	Racine dies
	Dryden dies
Boucher born; St Nicholas, Prague begun (Dietzenhofer brothers)	

	Music	History
1704	Biber dies; Charpentier dies; Handel in opera orchestra, Hamburg, working for Mattheson	allied forces under Marlborough defeat French at Blenheim; Newton's *Optics* published
1705	Farinelli born; Bach walks to Lübeck to hear Buxtehude; Handel's first opera *Almira* performed, Hamburg	Halley predicts (correctly) that a comet seen in 1682 will return in 1758
1706	Pachelbel dies; Handel goes to Italy	
1707	Buxtehude dies; Bach organist at Mühlhausen; Hotteterre publishes the first flute tutor	Act of Union joins England and Scotland in one kingdom
1708	Blow dies; Bach court organist at Weimar	
1709		Abraham Darby first smelts iron using coke; first successful imitation in Europe of Chinese porcelain
1710	Pergolesi born; Handel leaves Italy for Hanover, then London	
1711	Vivaldi Op. 3 Concertos, *L'estro armonico*; Handel's first opera for London, *Rinaldo*	royal porcelain factory opened at Meissen, Saxony
1712	Handel settles permanently in London	
1713	Corelli dies; François Couperin first book of *Pièces de clavecin*	Treaty of Utrecht: Spain loses possessions in Europe

Art and Architecture	Literature
Pozzo begins to decorate villa of Prince of Liechtenstein	Locke dies; Swift *A Tale of a Tub*; Antoine Gallaud begins first translation of *The Arabian Nights*
Luca Giordano dies; Blenheim Palace begun (Vanbrugh)	
	George Farquhar *The Beaux' Stratagem*
	Jean François Regnard *The Heir*
Hobbema dies	Samuel Johnson born
	Berkeley *Treatise Concerning the Principles of Human Knowledge*
	Nicholas Boileau dies; Hume born; Addison and Steele found *The Spectator*
	Rousseau born; Pope *Rape of the Lock*
	Diderot born; Scipione Maffei *Merope*

	Music	History
1714	C.P.E. Bach born; Gluck born; Vivaldi Op. 4 Concertos, *La stravaganza*	France cedes Spanish Netherlands to Austria; Fahrenheit makes a mercury thermometer
1715		Louis XIV of France dies
1716		
1717	Bach completes *Orgelbüchlein* before leaving Weimar to become Kapellmeister at Anhalt-Cöthen; Handel Water Music	
1718	Maurice Greene organist at St Paul's, London	
1719		
1720	D. Scarlatti takes up post at court in Lisbon; Benedetto Marcello *Il teatro alla moda*, a satire on Italian opera	financial disaster in England, the 'South Sea Bubble'; Lady Mary Wortley Montagu introduces smallpox inoculation
1721	Bach marries second wife Anna Magdalena; Telemann music director of five main churches in Hamburg	Russian victory over Sweden: Peter the Great proclaimed Emperor of all Russians
1722	Bach *Well-Tempered Clavier*, Book 1; Rameau *Traité de l'Harmonie*; Telemann director of Hamburg Opera	

Art and Architecture	Literature
	Leibniz *Monadology*
	Alain-René Lesage begins *Gil Blas*
Karlskirche, Vienna begun (Johann Fischer von Erlach)	Leibniz dies
Watteau *Pilgrimage on the Island of Cythera*	
	Defoe *Robinson Crusoe*
Piranesi born	
Watteau dies	
	Montesquieu *Lettres persanes*
	Defoe *Moll Flanders*

	Music	History
1723	Bach Cantor of Thomaskirche, Leipzig	
1724	Handel *Giulio Cesare*	
1725	A. Scarlatti dies; Philidor founds Concert Spirituel, Paris; Vivaldi Op. 8 published in Amsterdam, including *The Four Seasons*	St Petersburg Academy of Science founded
1726	Charles Burney born	
1727	war breaks out in London society between supporters of rival divas Faustina Bordoni and Francesca Cuzzon	
1728	Pepusch and Gay *The Beggar's Opera* a huge success in London	John Harrison designs marine chronometer
1729		
1730	Hasse Kapellmeister at Dresden	
1731	Hasse marries Faustina Bordoni	
1732	Haydn born; first public performance of Handel's oratorio *Esther*	
1733	F. Couperin dies; Telemann *Musique de Table*	

Art and Architecture	Literature
Wren dies; Joshua Reynolds born	Muratori begins *Rerum italicarum scriptores*, a monumental compilation of historical documents
	Metastasio *Didone abbandonata* (libretto)
	Giovanni Battista Vico Scienza nuova, a study of mankind's social evolution
Vanbrugh dies	Swift *Gulliver's Travels*; Voltaire in England
Gainsborough born	
Canaletto *The Stonemason's Yard*	Ephraim Chambers *Cyclopaedia*
	Defoe dies; Abbé Prévost *Manon Lescaut*
	Voltaire *Zaïre*
	Pope *Essay on Man*

	Music	History
1734	Bach *Christmas Oratorio*	
1735	J.C. Bach born; Rameau *Les indes galantes*	Linnaeus introduces his system for classifying plants and animals
1736	Pergolesi dies	Turkey at war with Russia
1737	Stradivari dies (aged 93)	Duchy of Tuscany comes under Habsburg control
1738		Papal bull issued against Freemasonry
1739	Benedetto Marcello dies; Mattheson *Der volkommene Capellmeister* puts forward doctrine of the 'affections'	
1740	C.P.E. Bach harpsichordist at court of Frederick the Great, Berlin; Haydn a treble at St Stephen's, Vienna; Handel concerti grossi, Op. 6	War of Austrian Succession; Emperor Charles VI succeeded by Maria Theresa; circumnavigation of the globe by Anson (to 1744)
1741	Vivaldi dies; Handel's last opera, *Deidamia*	Stockholm Academy of Science founded
1742	Handel *Messiah* (Dublin)	Celsius proposes centigrade measurement of temperature
1743	Boccherini born	Maria Theresa crowned queen of Bohemia

Art and Architecture	Literature
Hogarth *A Rake's Progress*	Voltaire *Lettres philosophiques*, in praise of liberty and tolerance
Holkham Hall, Norfolk designed (William Kent)	
Radcliffe Camera, Oxford designed (James Gibbs)	
	Richardson *Pamela*
	Hume *Treatise of Human Nature*
Summer Palace, St Petersburg begun (Bartolomeo Rastrelli)	
Hogarth *Marriage à la Mode*	
church of Vierzehnheiligen, Bavaria begun (Balthazar Neumann)	

Music	History
1744 Handel *Semele*	Frederick the Great of Prussia invades Saxony
1745 Bach *Well-Tempered Clavier*, Book 2	invention of Leyden jar for storing electricity
1746	
1747 Bach plays piano for Frederick the Great, composes the *Musical Offering* using a theme of the King	
1749	Treaty of Aix-la-Chapelle: Prussia emerges as major power; ruins of Pompeii discovered
1749 Handel *Susanna*; idem, *Solomon*	Empress Maria Theresa unites Austria and Bohemia
1750 Bach dies	

Art and Architecture	Literature
	Pope dies
	Swift dies
Goya born; Canaletto moves to England	
	Richardson *Clarissa*; Johnson begins work on his dictionary
Piranesi begins *Vedute di Roma* series; church of Ottobeuren, Bavaria begun (Johann Michael Fischer)	Montesquieu *De l'Esprit des Lois*
	Fielding *Tom Jones*
Tiepolo commissioned to decorate archbishop's palace at Würzburg	

Composers of the Baroque Era

Tomaso Albinoni (1671–1751)
(*b*. Venice, Italy; *d*. Venice, Italy)

Gregorio Allegri (1582–1652)
(*b*. Rome, Italy; *d*. Rome, Italy)

Thomas Augustine Arne (1710–1778)
(*b*. London, England; d. London, England)

Charles Avison (1709–1770)
(*b*. Newcastle upon Tyne, England; *d*. Newcastle upon Tyne, England)

Johann Sebastian Bach (1685–1750)
(*b*. Eisenach, Germany; *d*. Leipzig, Germany)

Heinrich Ignaz Franz von Biber (1644–1704)
(*b*. Wartenberg [now Stráž pod Ralskem], nr Reichenberg [now Liberec], Czech Republic; *d*. Salzburg, Austria)

William Boyce (1711–1779)
(*b*. London, England; *d*. London, England)

Dietrich Buxtehude (*c*. 1637–1707)
(*b*. Helsingborg, Sweden; *d*. Lübeck, Germany)

Giacomo Carissimi (1605–1674)
(*b*. Marino, nr Rome, Italy; *d*. Rome, Italy)

Francesco Cavalli (1602–1676)
(*b*. Crema, Italy; *d*. Venice, Italy)

Jacques Champion de Chambonnières (1601/2–1672)
(*b*. Paris, France; *d*. Paris, France)

Marc-Antoine Charpentier (1643–1704)
(*b*. in or nr Paris, France; *d*. Paris, France)

Arcangelo Corelli (1653–1713)
(*b*. Fusignano, Italy; *d*. Rome, Italy)

François Couperin (1668–1733)
(*b*. Paris, France; *d*. Paris, France)

Louis Couperin (c. 1626–1661)
(*b*. Chaumes-en-Brie, France; *d*. Paris, France)

Girolamo Frescobaldi (1583–1643)
(*b*. Ferrara, Italy; *d*. Rome, Italy)

Giovanni Gabrieli (1554/7–1612)
(*b*. Venice, Italy; *d*. Venice, Italy)

Francesco Geminiani (1687–1762)
(*b*. Lucca, Italy; *d*. Dublin, Ireland)

George Frideric Handel (1685–1759)
(*b*. Halle, Germany; *d*. London, England)

Reinhard Keiser (1674–1739)
(*b*. Teuchern, nr Weissenfels, Germany; *d*. Hamburg, Germany)

Henry Lawes (1596–1662)
(*b*. Dinton, Wiltshire, England; *d*. London, England)

William Lawes (1602–1645)
(*b*. Salisbury, England; *d*. Chester, England)

Jean-Baptiste Lully (1632–1687)
(*b*. Florence, Italy; *d*. Paris, France)

Alessandro Marcello (1669–1747)
(*b*. Venice, Italy; *d*. Venice, Italy)

Benedetto Marcello (1686–1739)
(*b.* Venice, Italy; *d.* Brescia, Italy)

Johann Mattheson (1681–1764)
(*b.* Hamburg, Germany; *d.* Hamburg, Germany)

Claudio Monteverdi (1567–1643)
(*b.* Cremona, Italy; *d.* Venice, Italy)

Johann Pachelbel (1653–1706)
(*b.* Nuremberg, Germany; *d.* Nuremberg, Germany)

Michael Praetorius (c. 1571–1621)
(*b.* nr Eisenach, Germany; *d.* Wolfenbüttel, Germany)

Henry Purcell (1659–1695)
(*b.* London, England; *d.* London, England)

Jean-Philippe Rameau (1683–1764)
(*b.* Dijon, France; *d.* Paris, France)

Alessandro Scarlatti (1660–1725)
(*b.* Palermo, Sicily; *d.* Naples, Italy)

Domenico Scarlatti (1685–1757)
(*b.* Naples, Italy; *d.* Madrid, Spain)

Samuel Scheidt (1587–1654)
(*b.* Halle, Germany; *d.* Halle, Germany)

Heinrich Schütz (1585–1672)
(*b.* Köstritz [now Bad Köstritz], nr Gera, Germany; *d.* Dresden, Germany)

Alessandro Stradella (1639–1682)
(*b.* Nepi, nr Viterbo, Italy; *d.* Genoa, Italy)

Jan Pieterszoon Sweelinck (1562–1621)
(*b.* Deventer, Netherlands; *d.* Amsterdam, Netherlands)

Giuseppe Tartini (1692–1770)
(*b.* Istria [now Piran, Istra], Slovenia; *d.* Padua, Italy)

Georg Philipp Telemann (1681–1767)
(*b.* Magdeburg, Germany; *d.* Hamburg, Germany)

Antonio Vivaldi (1678–1741)
(*b.* Venice, Italy; *d.* Vienna, Austria)

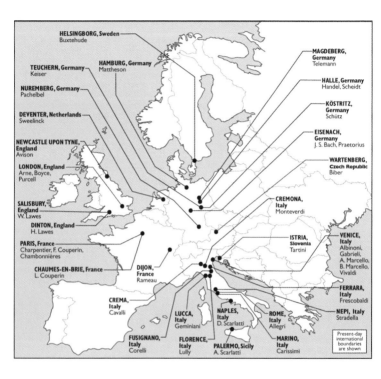

Map showing birthplaces of Baroque composers

Glossary

Anthem	choral piece intended as an extra item in a church service
Aria	a solo vocal piece in an opera, oratorio or cantata which is led by the melody rather than the text (see 'Recitative') and which gives opportunities for emotional and technical display
Bar (US: measure)	the visual division of metre into successive units, marked off on the page by vertical lines (barlines)
Beat	the unit of pulse (the 'throb' of the music)
Bridge	piece of wood attached to a string instrument to raise the strings and transmit their vibrations to the body of the instrument
Cantata	a work in several movements (arias, recitatives, duets etc.) for accompanied voice or voices, and on a smaller scale than an oratorio
Chaconne	a piece or movement based on a repeating ground bass, generally eight bars in length
Chord	any simultaneous combination of three or more notes
Claveciniste	harpsichord player
Clavier Übung	literally 'Keyboard Exercise'; most famously refers to a set of publications by Bach which borrows the title from Kuhnau and which includes the Six Partitas and the Goldberg Variations.

Concerto	a work generally for a solo instrument pitted against an orchestra, most commonly in three movements (fast–slow–fast)
Concerto grosso	a popular Baroque form based on the alternation of orchestra (known as the 'ripieno' or 'concerto') and a small group of 'soloists' ('concertino'); the most famous example is Bach's Brandenburg Concertos.
Continuo	a form of accompaniment in the seventeenth and eighteenth centuries, in which a keyboard instrument (most usually a harpsichord) harmonises the bass line played by the cello or viola da gamba
Counterpoint	the interweaving of separate 'horizontal' melodic lines, as opposed to the accompaniment of a top-line ('horizontal') melody by a series of ('vertical') chords
Courante	a Renaissance dance that became a regular ingredient of the Baroque suites. Most commonly a fast dance in triple time, it also occurs in a slower form with a more stately effect.
Da capo	literally 'from the beginning': an instruction to start again; it is frequently used in arias in Baroque music to create an A–B–A musical form, with the middle section generally contrasting in mood and key.
Equal temperament	tuning that divides the octave into equally sized intervals. Most western music since around 1700 uses this tuning system.
Fantasia	a free form, often of an improvisatory nature, following the composer's fancy rather than any preordained structures
Forte	loud
Fugue	a piece which is built entirely around imitative counterpoint. A fugue will usually consist of three or four instrumental or vocal strands (known as voices), based on a short tune (called the subject or theme) which is stated at the beginning by a single voice, and then taken up by the other voices and repeated in quick succession throughout the whole piece. Technically it is challenging for a composer and

historically the Baroque was a high point of fugal writing, with Bach the acknowledged master of the form.

Galliard a sprightly late-Renaissance dance in triple time of Italian origin (see 'Pavane')

Gavotte a dance of moderate pace and in duple time that became a mainstay of Baroque suites and ballet music

Ground bass a short bass pattern repeated throughout a section or entire piece; a famous example is 'Dido's Lament' from Purcell's *Dido and Aeneas.*

Harmony the simultaneous sounding of notes to make a chord; harmonies (chords) often serve as expressive or atmospheric 'adjectives', describing or giving added meaning to the notes of a melody.

Improvisation the act of creating music on the spot, without relying on any pre-existing music

Incidental music music used in the performance of a play

Invention a term for a short work, most famously associated with Bach who composed sets of fifteen two-part and three-part inventions

Kapellmeister chapel master (German)

Key pieces of western classical music are usually in particular keys, based on the notes of the western scale (C major, G minor etc.); a key is a piece's home – the music can travel away from it, but usually comes back in the end.

Lay clerk adult chorister

Lutheran chorale a hymn tune composed or arranged by Martin Luther, frequently in four-part harmony

Madrigal a vocal piece, generally for several voices and usually secular. Though the form flourished in the Renaissance, Monteverdi brought it to new heights with his sensitive word-setting and musical virtuosity.

Maestro di cappella	chapel master (Italian)
Maître de chapelle	chapel master (French)
Major	see 'Mode'
Masque	an allegorical entertainment typically including spoken verse, song and dance
Mass	the most solemn service of the Catholic Church, commemorating the Last Supper. By the Baroque the movements included were well-defined, namely Kyrie, Gloria, Credo, Sanctus and Agnus Dei.
Minor	see 'Mode'
Mode	the names given to a particular arrangement of notes within a scale. Every key in western classical music has two versions, the major and the minor mode; the decisive factor is the size of the interval between the key note (the tonic) and the third degree of the scale: if it is compounded of two whole tones (as in C–E [C–D/D–E]), the mode is major; if the third tone is made up of one and a half tones (C–E flat), the mode is minor. In general the minor mode is darker, more obviously dramatic than the major.
Modulation	the movement from one key to another, generally involving at least one pivotal chord common to both keys
Motet	a short sacred piece setting a single Latin text, for voices either unaccompanied or with organ
Musette	small bagpipe, used particularly in the operas of Lully and Rameau
Ode	a song form associated with particular celebratory occasions such as St Cecilia's Day. Purcell and Handel were particularly fine practitioners of the form.
Opera	basically, a sung play – a stage work that combines words, drama, music (with singers and orchestra), and often elaborate scenery

Oratorio an extended choral/orchestral setting of religious texts in a dramatic and semi-operatic fashion; the most famous example is Handel's *Messiah*.

Ordre suite

Ornament the embellishment of a note, originally as improvised by a performer

Overture an instrumental piece, commonly introducing an opera or oratorio. In Baroque times the term could also refer to a whole suite (Telemann's orchestral overtures being a case in point).

Partita originally 'variation', but more usually describing a suite, most famously Bach's partitas and sonatas for solo violin and his six keyboard partitas

Passion a musical setting of the Passion according to one of the four Evangelists, Matthew, Mark, Luke and John

Pastorale a lyrical instrumental or vocal piece imitating the music of shepherds. Typically it will have a lilting tempo and a tender melody.

Pavane a late-Renaissance dance of Italian origin, slow and processional in style and generally in duple metre; sometimes coupled with the more upbeat galliard

Piano soft

Pizzicato an instruction (first given by Monteverdi) to string players that a note should be plucked rather than bowed

Polyphony music with interweaving parts

Prelude literally, a piece which precedes and introduces another piece; but more generally it can mean a freestanding short piece, often of a semi-improvisatory nature.

Recitative a short narrative section in an opera, oratorio or cantata, usually sung by a solo voice accompanied by simple chords, generally preceding an aria. Rhythmically the style is free and determined by the text.

Ricercar   a contrapuntal work on a single theme

Scordatura   unorthodox tuning of a string instrument. It is used to create unusual harmonies or a particular musical effect – most spectacularly by Biber in his violin sonatas.

Semi-opera   a play with extensive musical content. Purcell wrote some of the most illustrious examples, including *King Arthur*, *The Fairy Queen* and *Dioclesian*.

Sonata   from the Italian for 'sounded', the term in the Baroque was fluid and could refer simply to relatively large forces, as in certain of Monteverdi's compositions. However, it gradually acquired a meaning with which we are familiar today, namely an instrumental work in up to four movements. Domenico Scarlatti ruled supreme where Baroque keyboard sonatas were concerned, writing well over 500.

Scale   from the Italian word *scala* ('ladder'); a series of adjacent, stepwise notes, moving up or down. Scales form the basis from which melodies are made and keys established.

Suite   a work in several short movements of contrasting styles, originally intended to be danced to. By the Baroque the suite had become divorced from the dance floor and typically included an allemande, courante, sarabande and gigue. Other movements were sometimes added (outstanding and eclectic examples exist by Bach, Handel, Rameau and François Couperin).

Tambourin   a rustic French dance in duple time imitating a pipe and tabor. Rameau frequently used them in his operas.

Toccata   a work most often for keyboard instruments at a fast tempo with a regular rhythm, demanding a virtuoso technique

Tombeau   a French genre used as a musical commemoration of a great performer or composer. Notable examples were written by Marais, Louis Couperin and D'Anglebert.

Tragédie en musique	French serious opera, usually used to describe works from the time of Lully to Gluck
Tremolo	Italian term for 'trembling': a rapid repetition of a single note through back-and-forth movements of the bow (on string instruments), or the rapid and repeated alternation of two notes (on keyboard or wind instruments)
Trill	the rapid alternation of two adjacent notes
Trio sonata	a sonata for two instruments (often violins) with continuo (i.e. keyboard instrument and either cello or viola da gamba)
Variation form	a musical form in which the melody (theme) is altered by elaboration, change of rhythm, key, tempo etc.
Verismo	term first used for Italian operas with an everyday setting but later extended to any opera in which the emotional temperature is consistently high
Violin makers	generic term for makers of string instruments
Word-painting	a setting of a word or text so that the meaning is reflected in the musical line

About the Author

Clive Unger-Hamilton was a professional harpsichordist before he entered the world of publishing and began to write about music. He is the author of several books on music history and related subjects, and writes regular reviews and other articles at home and abroad. He spent fourteen years living and working in France before moving to Ely with his wife and family, where he now works as a musicologist, editor and translator.

Index